# CLANS &
# TARTANS
## OF SCOTLAND & IRELAND

This edition published for
**Lomond Books Ltd, Broxburn, EH52, Scotland. 2010**

Publisher and Creative Director: Nick Wells
Project Editor: Chelsea Edwards
Art Director and Layout Design: Mike Spender
Digital Design and Production: Chris Herbert
Proofreader: Dawn Laker
Indexer: Geoffrey Meadon

Special thanks to Keith Lumsden, Trevor Maher and Donald W. Stewart.

**FLAME TREE PUBLISHING**
Crabtree Hall, Crabtree Lane
Fulham, London, SW6 6TY
United Kingdom

www.flametreepublishing.com

First published 2010

10 12 14 13 11
1 3 5 7 9 10 8 6 4 2

Flame Tree is part of the Foundry Creative Media Company Limited

© 2010 Flame Tree Publishing

ISBN 978 1 84204 249 6

A CIP record for this book is available from the British Library upon request.

All tartan images are courtesy of the Scottish Tartans World Register.
Pages 8–9 © V.K. Guy Ltd
Pages 310–11 © Panoramic Images/Getty Images

Every effort has been made to contact copyright holders. We apologize in advance for any omissions
and would be pleased to make any alterations in future editions of this publication.

Printed in China

# CLANS &
# TARTANS
## OF SCOTLAND & IRELAND

*Chris McNab*

**LOMOND**

# Contents

~

# Introduction

The clan system as we know it was a fusion of ancient Celtic tribalism and medieval feudalism, with earliest references appearing during the reign of David I (r. 1124–53). The word 'clan' comes from the Gaelic *clann*, meaning 'seed' or 'children'. In its pure form, the clan was a family grouping living in a defined territory and headed by a chief, with succession based on primogeniture or merit. Apart from the chief and his entourage, the clans were largely classless, which might explain how they survived well beyond the feudal era. The system meant that over time family names became inextricably linked to particular regions.

Indeed, clan identity became so strong that in *c*. 1746, following the Jacobite rebellions (the attempt to return the House of Stewart/Stuart to the British throne), the British government essentially banned the clan system and the wearing of tartan. But we must not overstate the rigidity of clan identities. Their origins frequently lay in Normandy, Scandinavia, England or Ireland, and could be fractured by feuds and divided loyalties. Clans might split into different territorial branches, while intermarriage frequently changed identity and allegiances. Yet ultimately, the clan system came to unite distinct groups of people under a common surname, the honour of which was stoutly defended.

So where does tartan fit into this picture? Tartan precedents were worn in ancient Celtic society, and we have documented references to tartans from the fifteenth century onwards. The setts (patterns) seem to have been based on territory, not name (or were specifically designed for certain military regiments), but that in itself would often link the pattern to a particular family. The link between surname and clan was largely a product of the early 1800s, defined with often dubious authenticity by publications such as James Logan's *The Scottish Gael* (1831) and the Sobieski brothers' *Vestiarium Scoticum* (1842), and also by major tartan manufacturers such as Wilsons of Bannockburn. The poet Sir Walter Scott (1771–1832), in his preparations for the visit of King George IV (r. 1820–30) to Scotland in 1822, had a formative influence on Scottish identity, strongly promoting tartan and clan history. Yet regardless of the origins of the clan/tartan relationship, it has endured.

Tartan is not just a Scottish affair. Ireland also has tartans, most being recent inventions to celebrate a particular county or family, and the setts are especially popular among people of Irish descent living abroad. Tartans sell in countries ranging from the United States to Japan, a surname being seen as a sufficient connection to Celtic culture. Many tartans are designed for specific individuals, companies, places or organizations, leading to literally hundreds of designs. This book presents some of the most popular, unusual and distinctive tartans, and in doing so reveals something of the history behind Scotland's great clans and Ireland's great regions.

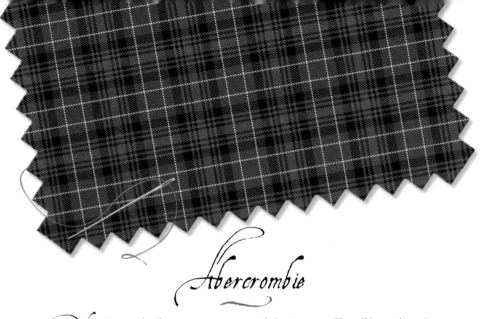

# Abercrombie

*Badge:* Acorned oak tree on a mount, with Latin motto *Tace* (Keep silence)

*Gaelic:* Obar Chrombaidh

The Abercrombie name derives from the barony of Abercrombie in Fife. Records of the Abercrombies date back to the thirteenth century – in 1296, William de Abercromby's allegiance to Edward I (*r.* 1272–1307) was stated in the Ragman Rolls. In the seventeenth century, William's line ended, but the Abercrombie name continued through the Birkenbog branch. Notable Abercrombies include the military leader Sir Ralph Abercromby (1734–1801), killed in Egypt fighting against Napoleon (1769–1821) in 1801, and his brother Robert (1740–1827), who became governor of Edinburgh Castle in the same year.

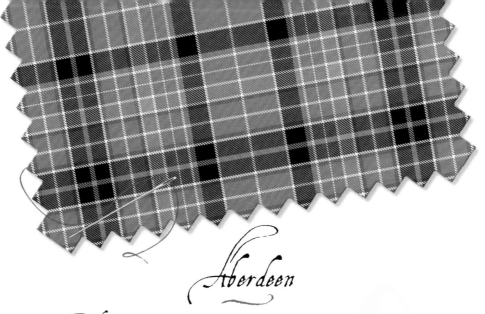

# Aberdeen

**Badge:** Three towers, with French motto *Bon accord* (Good agreement)
**Gaelic:** *Obar Dheathain*

Aberdeen was granted a city charter by William the Lion (r. 1165–1214) in 1179. In 1306, its citizens helped Robert the Bruce (r. 1306–29) enter Aberdeen Castle and kill the English occupants, the password used to enter the castle being *Bon accord*, which became the city's motto. Bruce's granting of the 'Great Charter' in 1319 made Aberdeen a financially independent entity. After Edward III burnt the city to the ground in 1336, it was rebuilt and named New Aberdeen. The tartan was registered in the late eighteenth century, by which time the city was prosperous and elegant.

## Agnew

*Badge:* Perched bird, with the Latin motto *Consilio non impetu* (By counsel, not force)
*Gaelic:* Ó Gnímh

The Agnew name in Scotland appears on historical records in 1190, when one William des Aigneau is recorded as a witness on a charter for Jedburgh Abbey, the French spelling of the name suggesting Norman origins. Some historians, however, argue that the Agnew family is derived from the O'Gnew of Ulster, migrants to Scotland during the medieval period. During the fourteenth and fifteenth centuries, Agnews provided the hereditary sheriffs of both Galloway and Wigtown, and Andrew Agnew was appointed the Constable of Lochnaw Castle in 1426.

# Alexander

*Gaelic:* Alasdair

Prior to the 1690s, the Alexander name had the 'Mac' suffix. The name had origins in European history, with antecedents in Alexander the Great (356–323 BC) and several Russian and Eastern European kings. The seat of the clan Alexander is Stirling, and the family played a significant role in the formation of modern Scotland and in Scottish acts of colonization. Sir William Alexander (*c.* 1570–1640), the 1st Earl of Stirling, was a driving force behind Scottish colonization in Nova Scotia and New York. His influence is seen today in the coat of arms and flag of Nova Scotia and even in the naming of Canadian coastguard cutters.

# Allison

**Motto:** *Vincit veritas* (Truth conquers)   **Gaelic:** *MacAlasdair*

Origins of the Allison name are uncertain and contentious. The clan may have been a branch of the Clan Donald through the sept of the MacDonalds known as the MacAlisters. There is evidence of Argyllshire MacAlisters settling in Lanarkshire and taking the name Allison. The name came in several varieties, including Ellis, Elson, Allasone, Alesoun and Ellison, and began appearing in extant documentation in the mid-thirteenth century. The family may first be attested in 1296, when Patrick Alissone of Berwick added his name to the Ragman Rolls.

# Anderson

**Badge:** Oak tree, with Latin motto *Spem successus alit* (Success nourishes hope; popularly 'Stand sure') **Gaelic:** MacGill'Anndrais

A branch of Inverness-shire Clan Chattan, the Andersons established themselves around Badenoch, a territory to which they moved from remote Moidart in *c.* 1400. From the 1500s, the Anderson clan have a particularly strong intellectual history, producing some major figures in the fields of science, mathematics and medicine. These include the mathematician Alexander Anderson (*c.* 1582–1620), known for his work in algebra and geometry, and Dr John Anderson (1726–96), a professor of natural philosophy at the University of Glasgow and a founding figure in the history of Strathclyde University.

## Angus

The name Angus enters the history books in the ninth century, although the Angus forename predates this. The clan claims its descent from Oenghus, the medieval King of Dalriada. His territory covered much of western Scotland and also parts of the north-east coast of Ireland. By the later Middle Ages, the Angus people had established a small fiefdom in eastern Scotland, and in 1320 the Angus lords were central to the Scottish Declaration of Independence at Arbroath. The Angus tartan is not name specific, and can be worn by anyone from the Angus region.

## Arbuthnott

**Badge:** Peacock's head, couped at the neck proper, with Latin motto *Laus Deo* (Praise God)

**Gaelic:** Obar Bhuadhnait

The Arbuthnott name derives from the Aberbothenoth, lands in Kincardineshire that passed into the possession of the Swintons, a border family, during the late twelfth century. It was Hugh de Swinton's son, Duncan, who took the Arbuthnott name, and during subsequent history the Arbuthnotts played frequently troubled roles in Anglo-Scottish politics. During the English Civil War, for example, Sir Robert Arbuthnott (*c.* 1620–55) was made 1st Viscount of Arbuthnott by Charles I (*r.* 1625–49), but nonetheless sided with the Covenanters – resulting in Royalists sacking his estate in 1645.

*Argyll*

*Badge:* A galley surmounted by a fess chequy, plus a gyronny and a wing holding a crowned sword, with Gaelic motto *Seas ar còir* (Maintain our right)  *Gaelic:* Earra-Ghàidheal

The territory of Argyll in western Scotland is intimately bound up with the history of the powerful Campbell clan and, perhaps unsurprisingly, the regional tartan is a variation of the Campbell sett. ('Sett' refers to the particular pattern of a tartan, determined by its vertical and horizontal colour and line arrangements.) As with many tartans, the Argyll pattern was a nineteenth-century creation, established by the venerable weavers Wilsons of Bannockburn in 1819. Being a regional tartan, it can be worn both by bearers of the family name and by anyone from Argyllshire.

# Armstrong

**Badge:** An arm embowed proper, with Latin motto *Invictus maneo* (I remain unvanquished)
**Gaelic:** MacGilleLàidir

The Armstrongs were a border clan known for their martial qualities and belligerence, and for lawless activities such as cattle rustling and cross-border raiding. They combined aggression with political power: one Gilbert Armstrong was King David II's ambassador to England during the fourteenth century. Such was their threat to stability that in 1530, James V (r. 1513–42) hanged the leader John Armstrong of Gilnockie along with 30 of his followers. The clan was terminally weakened by this event. The astronaut Neil Armstrong carried a fragment of the Armstrong tartan during his 1969 moon walk.

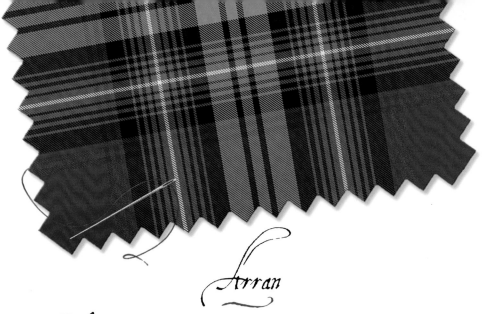

*Arran*

*Badge:* Fess between three cross-crosslets, with Latin motto *In hoc signo vinces* (In this sign conquer) *Gaelic:* Eilean Arainn

Another regional sett, the Arran tartan relates to the picturesque and popular Isle of Arran, off the western coast of Scotland. The island was inhabited from the Neolithic era and subsequently became a Viking settlement in the eleventh century AD. Yet the island's Gaelic heritage endured, and the language was still spoken on Arran up until the late twentieth century. On the western side of the island, some communities saw Gaelic spoken by more than 70 per cent of inhabitants in 1901, although that proportion fell dramatically over subsequent decades, and is today extinct.

## Atholl

**Badge:** Demi-savage with knife and key, with Old Scots motto 'Furth Fortune and Fill the Fetters' (Go onward with fortune and fill the shackles) **Gaelic:** Athall

The tartan of Atholl, a district in northern Perthshire, was designed in the seventeenth century. Yet the two great family names associated with the district – Murray and Stewart – go back well into the medieval period, with the earldom of Atholl given to Sir John Stewart in 1457, later passing to the Murrays. The Atholl closely resembles the Murray tartan, and the badge is of Murray derivation. Over the ages, three badges emerged from the Murray clan, including a mermaid holding a mirror. The modern demi-savage was actually the badge of the original Atholl Stewarts.

## Auld Reekie

'Auld Reekie', translating into English as 'Old Smokey', was the gritty nickname applied to Edinburgh from the sixteenth century. The label came from the massive amount of air pollution generated by the city's thousands of coal- and wood-burning fires, producing a smoke that clung in the streets and alleyways, and penetrated houses. The term became more widespread in the eighteenth century, after it was popularized in a poem by Robert Ferguson (1750–74). This tartan is thoroughly modern, designed in 1997 by Burkcraft Ltd for tourist consumption. Applied to a wide range of consumer goods, such tartans are general representatives of tartan work, rather than being connected to specific clan setts.

# Ayrshire

**Badge:** Castle, chevron, shakefork and fess chequy, with Scots motto *God schaw the richt*
**Gaelic:** *Siorrachd Àir*

Another regional tartan, this sett is designed to represent the perceived qualities of this south-western area of Scotland. While the green colours represent the rural landscape, gold signifies the region's productive farmland, blue the Irish Sea, black the coal industry, pale blue the districts of Kyle and Cunningham, and purple the district of Carrick. The tartan is a modern design, but the people of Ayrshire are rightly proud of their region's heritage. Two great figures of Scottish history – Robert the Bruce and Robert Burns (1759–96) – were both born in Ayrshire.

# Baillie

*Badge:* Boar's head, with Latin motto *Quid clarius astris?* (What is brighter than the stars?)
*Gaelic:* Bàillidh

The Baillie name comes from the position of 'bailie' (the word is the Scots equivalent of sheriff). Some historians claim that Baillie as a clan name originated after the Scottish king John Balliol (r. 1292–96) abdicated, resulting in many of his family making a name change to Baillie. The tartan was designed in the late 1700s, specifically for a military force – the Baillie Fencibles. This 600-strong regiment was created by Major Baillie of Duncan in 1794 with the onset of the French Revolutionary Wars and was based at Inverness.

# Baird

**Badge:** Eagle's head, with Latin motto *Dominus fecit* (The Lord made it)
**Gaelic:** Mac a' Bhàird (Son of the bard)

The Baird clan was established in Lanarkshire during the twelfth and thirteenth centuries. A legend goes that a man called Baird rescued William I (r. 1165–1214) when he was attacked by a wild boar. In gratitude, the king granted the man landholdings in Lanarkshire. An alternative history, however, argues that the Baird line was started by a Norman knight called Le Seigneur de Barde, who settled in Scotland following the Norman Conquest. Notable Bairds include General Sir David Baird (1757–1829) and the inventor John Logie Baird (1888–1946).

## Balfour

**Badge:** Three otters' heads, with Latin motto *Birtus ad aethera tendet* (Let valour reach out into the heavens)  **Gaelic:** *Baile Phùir*

The Balfour name originates in Fife, in the parish of Markinch. Prominent Balfours are mentioned as far back as the first decade of the fourteenth century and, from that period to the present day, the various strands of the clan have produced influential citizens. Luminaries include John Hutton Balfour (1808–84), a highly respected scientist and botanist, and the embryologist Francis Balfour (1851–82). Perhaps most remembered is Arthur James Balfour (1848–1930), who served as the British Prime Minister from 1902 to 1905 and Foreign Secretary from 1916 to 1919.

# Balmoral

*Gaelic:* Baile Mhoireil

The Balmoral tartan has distinctly royal origins. Royal interest in traditional Highland clothing, particularly tartans, stretches back to King George IV's (r. 1820–30) pomp-filled visit to Edinburgh in 1822. During the later reign of Queen Victoria (r. 1837–1901), Prince Albert designed a tartan and named it after the Balmoral residence in Aberdeenshire, which had come into the Prince's possession in 1852 and which has remained a royal Scottish residence to this day. Although initially created as a wall covering, the Balmoral tartan was adapted for clothing and was (and still is) worn by royals when visiting Scotland. It has also become popular as a general form of tartan amongst those without a clan name.

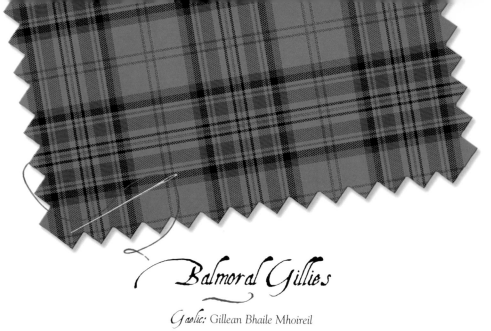

# Balmoral Gillies

*Gaelic:* Gillean Bhaile Mhoireil

Prince Albert's foray into tartan design set in train a series of variations, including tartans for day and evening wear. Another interesting variation emerged in the 1920s or 1930s, and is known as the 'Balmoral Gillies'. The term 'gillie' derives from the Gaelic 'boy' or 'servant', used for a gamekeeper or someone who acts as an attendant during a hunting or fishing trip. It originally referred to a Highland chief's attendant. The Gillie tartan was designed specifically for Highland servants, and the subdued colours reflect the need to avoid bright clothing when hunting in the field.

# Barclay

**Badge:** Out of a chapeau azure a hand holding a dagger, with Latin motto

*Aut agere aut mori* (Either action or death)

This venerable Scottish clan began, as with so many other Scottish clans, with Norman knights settling in Scotland following the Norman Conquest of 1066. The line commenced with Walter de Berkeley, who in 1165 was appointed Chamberlain of Scotland. The Barclays went on to produce high-profile leaders in the fields of military command, religious faith (particularly the Quakers) and banking. A Livonian branch of the Barclays, for example, yielded Russian Field Marshall Prince Michael Andreas Barclay de Tolly (1761–1818), who led Russian forces in the defeat of Napoleon in 1812.

## Baxter

*Motto:* Vincit veritas (Truth prevails)    *Gaelic:* Bacastair

Baxter derives from the Middle English word *bakstere*, meaning a baker. The humble profession, however, belies the high status of the Baxter clan in its early days. One Geffrie le Baxter of Forfar put his name to the oath of allegiance to Edward I in 1296, while the Dundee Baxters had a formative effect on the wealth generation and development of the city – David Baxter (1793–1872), for example, gave the city the 36-acre Baxter Park in 1863. The well-known modern brand of Baxter's soups and preserves comes from the Fochabers line. Other prominent Baxters include the theologian Richard Baxter (1615–91) and the inventor of the ink roller, John Baxter (1781–1856).

# Bell

*Badge:* Hand holding a dagger, with the Scots motto *I beir the bel*

The Bell clan occupied the Scottish borderlands of Dumfriesshire even before the Norman Conquest of 1066 and, during the late Middle Ages, became known as a particularly restless clan. (Note that the name appears in various other forms, such as Bel, Bellis, Belle, Beall, Beal, Beale and Bale.) King James's Act of 1587 lists the Bell clan as one of those exercising independent patriarchal rule outside of the English feudal system. The Bells were also known for their alliance with the Douglases, often accompanying them on cross-border raids. The seventeenth and eighteenth centuries, however, saw a broad exodus from traditional Bell lands, as population growth strained local agricultural production.

# Berwick-upon-Tweed

*Badge:* Bear tied to a wych-elm, with Latin motto *Victoria gloria merces*
(Valour rewards with glory)   *Gaelic:* Bearaig

Berwick-upon-Tweed has arguably the most vibrant and troubled history of any British town. Its location just 4 km (2 miles) south of the (modern) Scottish border, at the mouth of the River Tweed, placed it on the frontline of the Anglo-Scottish wars. The town swapped hands at least 13 times during the Middle Ages, and attracted the wrath of Edward I in 1296, who slaughtered all its inhabitants. Despite its bloody history, Berwick was nevertheless a centre of thriving national and international trade, and it took the Act of Union in 1707, finally settling ownership in England's favour. The town remains, however, distinctively Scottish in many elements of outlook and culture.

## Bethune

*Badge:* Demi-otter, with the motto 'Debonnaire'  *Gaelic:* Peutan

The Bethune clan began with an influx of Anglo-Norman settlers from the village of Bethune in Pas-de-Calais, France, during the eleventh and twelfth centuries. Settling in Fife and Angus, the Bethune clan also produced a clan Beaton offshoot famed for their medical skills, and the two names became thoroughly mixed in the Lowlands of Scotland. Some Beatons/Bethunes became septs of the more powerful Clan MacLeod, although one branch of the Bethunes retained its independence from its powerful neighbour. Many Bethunes later emigrated to Canada; a prominent Canadian Bethune was the surgeon Norman Bethune (1899–1939), known for his combat surgery in the Spanish Civil War and Second Sino-Japanese War.

## Black Watch

**Badge:** St Andrew within a wreath of thistles, on the star of the Order of the Thistle, with Latin motto *Nemo me impune lacessit* (No one attacks me with impunity)  **Gaelic:** Am Freiceadan Dubh

The Black Watch is the Royal Highland Regiment, a prestigious formation of the British Army founded back in 1739 when George II amalgamated six Highland 'Watch' companies. The purpose of the original companies was essentially to keep the peace for the government in the Highlands, and they were visually distinguished by the tartan pattern that endures to this day. (The 'Black Watch' title derives from the dark shades of the tartan.) The regiment served with distinction for 266 years, before becoming a battalion within the Royal Regiment of Scotland in 2006.

## Blair

**Badge:** Bird with spread wings, with Latin motto *Virtute tutus* (Protected by valour)
**Gaelic:** Blàr

The Blair name appears during the medieval period in several regions, particularly Renfrew, Ayr, Perth, Fife and Angus. One early reference is the granting of a Barony of Blair in Ayrshire by King William I, the Lion (r. 1165–1214) in the second half of the twelfth century. Spelling variations abounded – there were no fewer than 16 – but today, three principal variations remain: Blair, McBlair and Bleher. The name has military connotations, the Gaelic *blàr* meaning both field and battlefield. Probably the most famous modern Blair is former Prime Minister Tony Blair.

## Blue

*Gaelic:* MacGilleGhuirm

According to the current Scottish Register of Tartans, 'Anyone can submit an application to register a tartan'. For the registration to be successful, the tartan must be unique (distinguishable from others with the naked eye), and typically should have a clear rationale behind its creation, such as to celebrate a particular event, promote a district or add to existing clan tartans. The Blue tartan here is an attractive example of relatively modern registrations. Featuring broad blue bands accented by thin red and white lines, the sett was designed by Jamie Scarlett MBE for the family of one American historian, Douglas Kelly, in the United States and registered in 1985.

## Borthwick

*Badge:* Moor's head, with Latin motto *Qui conducit* (He who serves)

The Borthwick clan claims a particularly venerable ancestry on the Scottish borders: legend has it that they resisted Roman intrusions during the first century AD. More concrete evidence emerges of Borthwick ancestors in the Anglo-Saxon period (410–1066), with references to Borthwick nobles fighting the Saracens in the early Crusades. The ancestral lands of Borthwick Water in Roxburghshire were held by charter in the fifteenth century by William de Borwick, Captain of Edinburgh Castle. Mary Queen of Scots (r. 1542–57) sheltered in Borthwick Castle in 1567 when it was besieged by rebels, but escaped dressed as a boy. Her ghost is said to linger there still.

## Bowie

*Gaelic:* Buidhe

Jim Bowie (1796–1836), defender of the Alamo and inventor of the Bowie Knife is probably one of the best known Bowies. Looking much further back, however, we find several Bowie (or Bowey, Boway and Bowye) figures in the service of or in opposition to the royals. The rebel John Bowey resisted the forces of James IV (r. 1488–1513) in 1489, although was later given remission. There is a reference to one Andrew Bowye serving as a notary public in Scone in 1570, and a Jerome Bowie was a keeper of the royal wine cellars in the mid- to late-1580s.

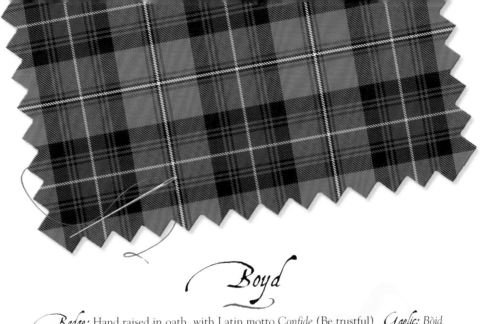

# Boyd

**Badge:** Hand raised in oath, with Latin motto *Confide* (Be trustful) **Gaelic:** Bòid

The Boyd name firmly enters the history books in 1263, when Boyds are recorded as leaders during the Battle of the Largs against Scandinavian invaders. Sir Robert Boyd served Robert the Bruce (r. 1306–29) at the Battle of Bannockburn in 1314, for which he gained substantial landholdings in Kilmarnock and Ayrshire. Despite the early traditions of resistance to British rule, the Boyds entered the peerage in 1454. Thomas Boyd (d. *c.* 1472) became the Earl of Arran in 1467, and one William Boyd (1646–92) became Earl of Kilmarnock in 1661.

## Braveheart Warrior

This tartan is a very recent invention, designed by Michael King for the Scottish martial arts champion, Ronnie Watt, also known as Braveheart Warrior. Watt used this name while he took part in an international competition in Japan. It was not designed for the film *Braveheart*, which incorrectly depicts Mel Gibson's William Wallace wearing tartan, but has since been associated with the film because of the name. Though the Braveheart name is now inextricably linked with the historical figure of William Wallace there is no evidence to suggest that it was ever used to describe him prior to the film's release.

## Brodie

*Badge:* Hand gripping three arrows, with motto 'Unite'   *Gaelic:* Brothaidh

The Brodie name likely comes from the Pictish 'Brude', an ancient tribe of Morayshire. Although early records are scarce – many archives were lost when Brodie Castle burnt to the ground in 1645 – we know of a Malcolm, Thane of Brodie, in the time of Alexander III (r. 1249–86), and that his son Michael received a charter from Robert Bruce just prior to the Battle of Bannockburn. Brodies became influential in UK affairs. Alexander Brodie of Brodie (1617–79) helped with the return of Charles II (r. 1660–85), and negotiated with Oliver Cromwell (1599–1658) over Anglo-Scottish union in 1651.

## Brown

*Badge:* Lion rampant, with Latin motto *Floreat majestas* (Let majesty flourish)
*Gaelic:* MacGilleDhuinn

The name Brown, or Broun, is thought to be a French import – 'Le Brun'. By the twelfth century, 'Brown' was appearing in Scottish records. A Walterus Brown was a religious leader in Glasgow around 1116, and one Richard de Broun signed the Ragman Rolls in 1296. A particularly venerable line of Brouns are the Brouns of Coulston, whose powerful descendants occupied positions ranging from the High Sheriff of Aberdeenshire to the Provost of Dundee. This line claims its origins in the royal house of France, hence the three French gold lilies on its arms.

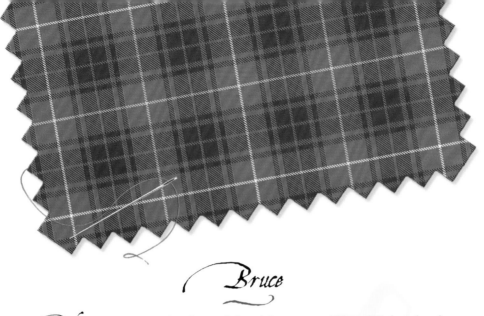

## Bruce

*Badge:* Lion statant with tail extended, with Latin motto *Fuimus* (We have been)
*Gaelic:* Brus

The Bruce story begins with the Norman Conquest of 1066, after which the Norman family of de Brus became associated with David I of Scotland (r. 1124–53). The Bruces went on to become a powerful family in Scottish politics, and are known for their resistance to the imposition of English rule, the family even having claims to the throne of Scotland through the marriage of the 4th Lord of Annandale (Robert) to the niece of William the Lion. The 7th Lord of Annandale, the famous Robert the Bruce, is the legendary victor of Bannockburn in 1314.

# Bruce of Kinnaird

*Gaelic:* Brusach a' Chinn Àird

Over the centuries, the Bruce clan has produced many offshoots, the Bruce of Kinnaird being a well-respected line. The first of the line was Sir Alexander Bruce, who bought the lands of Kinnaird House in 1476. Famous Bruces of this line include Robert Bruce (1554–1631) and James Bruce (1730–94). Robert was an influential theologian and preacher, who was at first favoured and then exiled by James VI (1567–1625), but was allowed to return to preaching in Scotland by Charles I (r. 1625–49). James Bruce was a remarkable eighteenth-century explorer, who travelled through Abyssinia and found the source of the Blue Nile, but died after falling down the steps at Kinnaird House.

# Buccleuch

*Badge:* Stagg trippant proper, with Latin motto *Amo* (I love)

Buccleuch is a branch of the Scott clan (*see* page 280). The lives of the Buccleuchs were often intimately interwoven with affairs of state and royalty. The lordship of Scott of Buccleuch was created in 1606 and later in the seventeenth century, Anne, Countess of Buccleuch, married the Duke of Monmouth, the illegitimate son of King Charles II (*r.* 1660–85). The Duke of Buccleuch peerage was established in 1663 and survives to this day. The Buccleuchs have two types of tartan: a regimental version worn by the King's Own Scottish Borderers, and a version designed in 1830 in tribute to Sir Walter Scott.

## Buchan

*Badge:* Three lions' heads with Latin motto *Non inferiora secutus* (Not having followed inferior things)

*Gaelic:* Bùchainn

The Buchan name comes from the Aberdeenshire region of Buchan. The first ancestor to appear in extant records is Ricardus de Buchan in 1207, by which time the earldom of Buchan was actually in the hands of the Comyns family – the fortunes of the two families have remained intertwined ever since. Significant figures of the Buchan family include Thomas Buchan of Auchmacoy, a great Scottish military leader during the seventeenth and eighteenth centuries, and the twentieth-century novelist, politician and Governor General of Canada, John Buchan (1875–1940).

## Buchanan

*Badge:* Hand holding up a ducal coronet, set within a laurel wreath, with Latin motto *Clarior hinc honos* (Brighter, hence the honour)   *Gaelic:* Bochanan

The Buchanan family has Irish ancestry. The Irish chieftain Anselan O'Kyan settled in Argyll in the early eleventh century, and was rewarded the Buchanan lands east of Loch Lomond for his services to King Malcolm II (r. 1005–34). These lands stayed in the family for the next four hundred years. The Buchanans were staunchly anti-English. Sir Alexander Buchanan fought for the French at the Battle of Baugé in 1421 – his killing of the Duke of Clarence, after which he took the duke's coronet as a trophy, is ostensibly the inspiration behind the Buchanan badge.

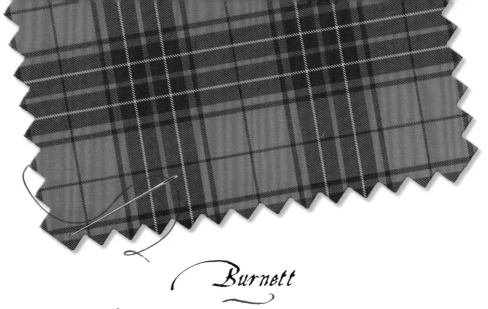

## Burnett

*Badge:* Arm pruning a vine, with Latin motto *Virescit vulnere virtus*
(Courage flourishes with a wound)

One account of the Burnett clan traces its origins back to the Beornhard ('bear hand', later Burnard) family, which attended on David I (r. 1124–53). Another theory has the name deriving from the French 'Burnet'. Following the Norman Conquest, they settled in Roxburghshire, but their support of Robert the Bruce (r. 1306–29) brought expanded holdings in Kincardineshire and the Forest of Drum. Since then, the Burnetts have split into numerous septs and branches, and have produced many influential personalities in military command, the law and politics.

## Burns

**Badge:** Tree over a shepherd's crook and stock horn, with the motto
'Better a wee bush than nae bield' (shelter)

Burns is an extremely common surname in Scotland, deriving from the Old English *burna* (brook) or 'burn-house' (a house by a brook). More of a family name than a distinct clan, Burns descendants have separated out into numerous branches, with some branches able to verify their ancestry all the way back to the fourteenth century (such as the Burns of Glebervie district, Kincardineshire). Because of its familial diversification, Burns tartans have been a relatively recent act of standardization – the predominant Burns tartan, shown here, actually dates from the first half of the twentieth century.

## Burns, Robert

The poet Robert Burns (1759–96), revered as national poet of Scotland, holds such a significant place in Scottish culture that there is an individual tartan in his honour. (It is not unprecedented for individuals to receive their own tartans; other beneficiaries include Prince Albert and Sir Walter Scott.) This specific check was designed by the Belgian lord Baron Georges Marchand, at the request of *The Scotsman* newspaper to honour the bicentenary of the great poet. As Burns himself was from the Lowlands (he was born in Alloway, Ayrshire) and was a farmer, the pattern was modelled on a shepherd's traditional garb, with subtle greys and greens.

# Caledonia

*Gaelic:* Cailleann

The Caledonia tartan is another generic Scottish tartan. It was created by the famous Wilsons of Bannockburn in 1819 (*see* page 307), and given a name in memory of the fierce Caledonii tribe that so plagued the Romans. 'Caledonia' was actually the name given to Scotland by the Romans, at least the Scotland north of Hadrian's Wall. (All the territory to the south of the wall was called Britannia.) Once the Romans left Britain, the Caledonia name fell dormant, until revived in the eighteenth century as another name for the Scottish nation. The revival took hold, and the Caledonia name is today used in many commercial titles, sports clubs and other institutions.

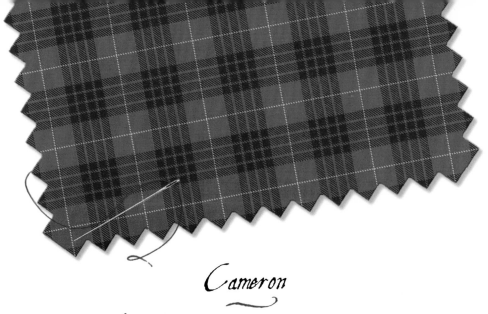

## Cameron

*Badge:* Arm clad in armour, displaying a sword, with Latin motto
*Pro rege et patria* (For king and country)  *Gaelic:* Camshron

The Camerons were a powerful and warlike clan. They were reputed to be exceptionally fierce in battle, as attested to by their Gaelic war cry: *Chlanna nan con thigibh a so's gheibh sibh feoil* (Sons of the hounds come here and get flesh). By the early fifteenth century, the Cameron chief Donald Dubh oversaw a confederation with three principal septs: the MacMartins of Letterfinlay, the MacSorleys of Glen Nevis and the MacGillonies of Strone. As their motto indicates, the Camerons were royalist by tendency, serving the Stewart kings during the seventeenth century.

# Cameron of Erracht

**Badge:** St Andrew holding a saltire cross   **Gaelic:** Camshronach Eireachd

The Camerons of Erracht were born through marriage, when Ewen Cameron of Lochiel (son of Allan, thirteenth chief of the Camerons) married Marjory Mackintosh in the sixteenth century. By this time, relations between the Camerons and the Mackintoshes were fraught, and the marriage did not heal this situation. One of Marjory and Ewen's offspring, another Ewen, went on to form the Erracht branch of the Camerons. The tartan that we see here was designed by Sir Allan Cameron of Erracht (commander of the 79th Cameron Highlanders) and his mother during the late eighteenth century.

## Cameron of Lochiel

*Badge:* Five arrows tied together, with Gaelic motto *Aonaibh ri chéile* (Unite together)

*Gaelic:* Camshronach Loch Iall

The Cameron of Lochiel title was established in 1528, when James V (r. 1513–42) granted the name Captain of Clan Cameron in a royal charter. The clan chiefs that followed were often formidable warriors. The 17th chief (Ewen) fought for the Royalists during the Civil War, but he was also a diplomat, bringing the centuries-old feud with the Mackintoshes to an end. His grandson, 'Gentle Lochiel', fought for the Jacobites, for which he was eventually forced to flee to France. Other Camerons gained distinction in later battles during the Napoleonic and world wars.

## Campbell

**Badge:** Boar's head, with Latin motto *Ne obliscaris* (Do not forget)  **Gaelic:** *Caimbeul*

The Campbells are one of the great Scottish clans. During the High and Late Middle Ages, they established dominance in Argyllshire, with authority extending to the Western Highlands and the Hebrides. The actual origins of the name are uncertain. The most likely Celtic theory suggests that the Campbells are derived from the Irish warrior-chief Diarmuid Ó Duibhne, known as *cam-beul* (wry mouth) on account of his crooked expression. Alternatively, the Campbell name may have come from the marriage of Malcolm MacDiarmid with the Norman Beauchamp family in the eleventh century, *Beauchamp* translating into Latin as *de Campo Bello*.

# Campbell of Argyll

*Badge:* Boar's head, with Latin motto *Ne obliviscaris* (Do not forget)

*Gaelic:* Caimbeulach Earra-Ghàidheal

Over its first 400 years, the Campbell clan became divided into three main branches – the Cawdor, Breadalbane and Argyll Campbells – which, by the sixteenth century, produced relations bordering on outright hostility. It was largely the efforts of Archibald (c. 1575–1638), 7th Earl of Argyll, that kept the Campbells together, the Argyll branch becoming dominant. The clan chief is known as *Mac Cailein Mór* (Son of Colin the Great) after the warrior Colin of Lochawe, and the various earls and dukes of Argyll were prominent in British politics and military leadership well into the nineteenth century.

# Campbell of Breadalbane

*Badge:* Boar's head, with the motto 'Follow me'  *Gaelic:* Caimbeulach Bhràghaid Albann

Although the Earl of Breadalbane title died out in the 1920s, the Breadalbane Campbells for many centuries wielded significant power across Scotland, their influence at times rivalling that of the Argyll branch. The forerunner of the Breadalbane Campbells was Sir Colin of Glenorchy (1499–1583), a warrior and landowner responsible for building Kilchurn Castle (Loch Awe) and Balloch Castle (Loch Tay). In 1681, Sir John Campbell (1636–1717) was created the Earl of Breadalbane. This title survived until the twentieth century, when an absence of an heir brought it to an end.

# Campbell of Cawdor

*Badge:* A crowned swan, with the motto 'Be mindful'  *Gaelic:* Caimbeulach Chaladair

The Cawdor branch of the Campbells was born out of the marriage of Sir John Campbell (d. 1546), son of the second Earl of Argyll, to Muriel, daughter of the 7th Thane of Cawdor, and this title passed through to their grandson John Campbell (d. *c.* 1642). The Campbell of Cawdor tartan was actually branded an Argyll tartan in 1789 (it previously did not have a name). It received the official Campbell of Cawdor name in 1850, and is today one of the four Campbell tartans officially approved by the chief of the Campbells.

## Carlisle

*Badge:* A lion statant gardant, with Latin motto *Volo non valeo* (I am willing if not able)

The Carlisle tartan seen here is a creation of tartan designer Christopher Carlisle Justus, a native of Hendersonville, North Carolina. It is one of seven tartans designed by Justus during the 1980s. At the time of writing, three of these tartans are listed on the Scottish Register of Tartans: Justus Black and Gold (Angus) (Personal); Justus Dress (Personal); and Justus Hunting (Personal). The ability to create new tartans is part of the vitality of tartan history, and shows that tartans can represent personal as well as clan traditions.

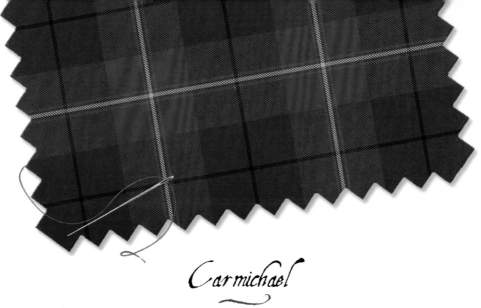

## Carmichael

*Badge:* A hand holding a broken lance, with French motto *Toujour prest* (Always ready)

*Gaelic:* MacGilleMhìcheil

The Carmichael seat is in Lanarkshire. The barony of these lands was granted to William, Earl of Douglas (1327–84) but, in the *c.* 1370s, it passed to Sir John Carmichael, James Douglas's nephew. The Carmichaels fought the English in France during the Hundred Years' War – the badge's image of a broken lance is said to come from the English commander Clarence, whose lance was snapped at the Battle of Baugé in 1421 when he was unseated by Sir John Carmichael. During the Civil Wars of the 1640s, however, Carmichaels fought on both sides.

## Carnegie

**Badge:** Winged thunderbolt, with the motto 'Dred God'

The Carnegie clan takes its name from the barony of Carnegie, in south-east Angus, granted to John de Balinhard in 1358. Further land was acquired by the Carnegies in Kinnaird during the late sixteenth century, but in the eighteenth century the Carnegies were stripped of their estates and titles after they had sided against the British during the Jacobite rebellion. These titles and lands were given back in the mid-nineteenth century. Andrew Carnegie (1835–1919) was an industrialist and philanthropist who emigrated to the USA and became one of the richest men in history.

## Caseley

The Caseley family tartan is another modern sett. Its story begins in 1990, when a Mr Gordon Caseley petitioned the Scottish Tartans Society (STS) for a new tartan design. Produced by Harry Lindley, the design demonstrated a striking patternsof reds, greens, blues and yellows. The sett was submitted to the accreditation process, and it received its official acceptance with the STS in 1993. The design is now registered on the Scottish Register of Tartans, a national repository of tartan designs run by the National Archives of Scotland, in turn an executive agency of the Scottish government. Launched in February 2009, the Register also vets and approves new tartan applications.

## Celtic F.C.

Given the near-religious status commanded by the Celtic Football Club amongst its fans, it was only natural that the club would acquire its own tartan. The club started up in 1888 as part of a Catholic missionary effort in Glasgow, but it rose to become a Scottish Premier League leader, battling it out with its main rival, Rangers. To give the Celtic supporters a uniform element of dress and celebrate the centenary of the club, a new tartan was designed by Tartan Sportswear, using the colour scheme of the players' uniforms. The sett was launched in 1989, but has been replaced by another sett following Tartan Sportswear's bankruptcy.

## Childers

The Childers tartan exists in two main versions: an original nineteenth-century version worn by the 1st Battalion, 1st Gurkha Rifles, and a modern (1997) family version. The former was the brainchild of Hugh C.E. Childers (1827–96), who served as the Secretary of War from 1880 to 1882. Following a series of controversial mergers, he attempted to introduce a tartan that would be adopted across all the Highland regiments. This did not happen but, in 1907, a variation of the tartan was designed by H.B. Mackintosh of Elgin for the War Office, who used the Mackintosh tartan as his basis. This tartan went to the Gurkhas, where it was used for decorative features such as ribbons and bag covers.

## Chisholm

*Badge:* A hand holding a dagger, transfixing a boar's head, with Latin motto
*Feros ferio* (I am fierce with the fierce) *Gaelic:* Siosalach

The story behind this clan's badge is that the Chisholm ancestors saved a king from the charge of a wild boar, and in gratitude he granted them their ancestral lands. Such stories are common in clan legend, so should be treated largely as myth. In fact, the Chisholms were of Norman extraction, and settled in Chieseholme, Roxburghshire, in the mid-thirteenth century, moving further north into the Highlands during the fifteenth and sixteenth centuries. The seat of the Chisholm clan chief was Erchless Castle, near Beauly in Inverness-shire.

## Christie

*Gaelic:* MacGilleChrìosd

The Christie clan originated around Stirling and Fife during the fifteenth century, the first reference being to one John Christie, an official of the town of Newburgh, in 1457. To this day, the surname is prevalent in Scotland, particularly around the traditional Christie lands; the name itself is probably a contraction of the forenames Christian or Christopher. Note that the Christies are classed as a sept of the Farquharsons (*see* page 103), a prominent Aberdeenshire clan. Prior to the twentieth century, notable Christies included James Christie of Perth (1730–1803), founder of the famous auction house. Within the twentieth century, the athlete Linford Christie and actress Julie Christie have given prominence to the name.

# Clan Chattan

**Badge:** Cat, with the motto 'Touch not the cat bot (without) a glove'
**Gaelic:** Clann Ghille Chatain

During the clans' frequent struggles with the government, and with each other, it often became advisable to form confederations. The Clan Chattan was such an alliance. It was originally an independent clan, but intermarriage with the Mackintosh clan resulted in one Angus Mackintosh taking the chieftainship of both clans in the fourteenth century. Territorial growth and further conflicts meant that other clans soon joined the growing confederation, which, by the end of the century, eventually numbered 17 clans. It was only in 1942 that the Mackintosh and Chattan chieftainships were separated.

# Clark

**Badge:** Unicorn's head  **Gaelic:** Mac a' Chléirich

An extremely common name, English Clark and Gaelic *cléireach* are both derived from the Latin *clericus*, meaning 'clerk' or 'scribe', fusing the acts of writing and religious devotion. Given its prevalence, it is inevitable that many Clarks have left their name on history. Richard Clark of Montrose was created a vice-admiral in the Swedish Navy in 1623 (indicating the close relationship between Scotland and Scandinavia), while General Mark Clark (1896–1984) made a controversial name for himself commanding US Army forces in the Second World War.

## Cochrane

**Badge:** Prancing horse, with Latin motto *Virtute et labore* (By valour and hard work)

The Cochranes are a particularly old Scottish clan, with an ancestry dating back to the Vikings, from whom many Cochrane historians claim the clan is descended. Certainly, Cochrane settlements were established around Renfrewshire during the tenth century, and direct text references appear during the 1260s. The name is sometimes derived from a Gaelic word for 'battle cry', but is more likely to come from the lands of Coueran near Paisley. During the seventeenth century, the Cochrane family entered into the peerage and – true to their reputation as the 'fighting Cochranes' – the family produced many high-ranking military leaders.

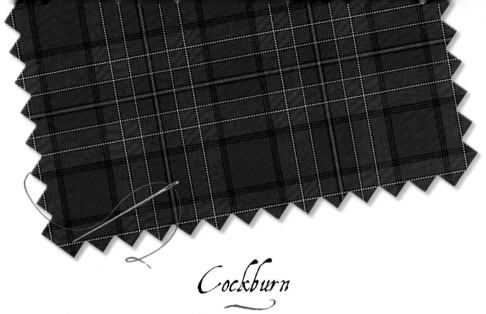

# Cockburn

*Badge:* A cock crowing, with Latin motto *Accendit cantu* (He is awakened by his singing)

The Cockburns (pronounced 'Coburn') date back to at least the thirteenth century (one Sir Pere de Cockburne signed the Ragman Rolls in 1296). A leading figure in the early history of the clan was Sir Alexander de Cockburn, who expanded the Cockburn territories in Berwickshire by marrying into the Langtons. His grandson Alexander was given the barony of Carriden in 1358 and became the Keeper of the Great Seal in 1389. Later famous Cockburns were Sir George Cockburn (1772–1853), an admiral in the Royal Navy, and Lord Chief Justice Sir Alexander Cockburn (1802–80).

# Colquhoun

**Badge:** Hart's head, with French motto *Si je puis* (If I can)   **Gaelic:** *Mac a' Chombaich*

During the reign of Alexander II (r. 1214–49), the lands of Colquhoun in Dumbartonshire were granted to Humphrey of Kilpatrick, an act that laid the foundations of the Colquhoun clan (Humphrey's son, Ingram, first took the name). The influence of the Colquhouns grew through judicious marriages, bringing the acquisition of the lands of Luss and the subsequent chieftainship over both Colquhoun and Luss territories. The beginning of the seventeenth century saw a long-standing rivalry between the Colquhouns and the MacGregors explode into murderous violence, which resulted in the MacGregor name being outlawed by the king.

# Commonwealth Games

*Gaelic:* Geumannan a' Cho-fhlaitheis

Many tartans have been created with a particular celebratory function in mind. The last thirty years have seen numerous such additions, of which the 'Commonwealth' tartan is one. It was designed in 1985 by Mrs L.P.G. Dow of Edinburgh, in response to a commission to design a tartan for the 1986 Commonwealth Games, which was staged in the Scottish capital. Produced by the Lochcarron company of Scotland, it was worn by staff at the Games. Eight years later, another tartan was designed, this time for the Scottish representatives at the 2006 Commonwealth Games in Melbourne, Australia. The design seen here was created by Kinloch Anderson Ltd.

# Connel

**Badge:** Boar's head, framed by two wings    **Gaelic:** Conaill

The Connel name, meaning 'strong as the wolf', has several possible origins. A popularly held derivation is the legendary Celtic warrior Conall Cernach, the name travelling from Ireland to Scotland during the early Middle Ages. Alternatively, it could be derived from the Celtic saint Comgall (c. 510–c. 600), who established a monastery at Bangor, County Down, during the sixth century. Either way, Connel, or variations such as Congallus or Conall, was established in Scotland during the early Middle Ages, making it one of the oldest clan names in the country.

## Cooper

Badge: Lion's jamb between sprigs of holly, with Latin motto *onata perficio*
(I perfect by undertakings)  Gaelic: Mac a' Chùbair

The Scottish Register of Tartans lists, at the time of writing, a total of five tartans associated with the Cooper name. These range from a dress tartan produced in 1998, a variation of an earlier nineteenth-century tartan, through to a special tartan designed for the Coopers & Lybrand company in 1996. The surname, however, is far older, dating back to at least the thirteenth century, with variations that include Cupar, Coupar and Cowper. The family lands are centred in Fife and Perthshire, the lands in Fife becoming a royal burgh in the fourteenth century.

## Coronation

*Gaelic:* Crùnadh

This sett was designed for a royal coronation event – that of King George VI (*r.* 1936–52) in 1936. The Scottish Register of Tartans actually lists two tartans designed for this event. Both of them are rendered in the red, white and blue of the Union Flag, although the second has broader lines. Both, however, have red as the dominant background colour, evoking the Stewart tartan. An interesting historical note is that the tartan was originally designed for the coronation of Edward VIII (*r.* 1936), but his relationship with the American Wallis Simpson resulted in his abdication in December 1936.

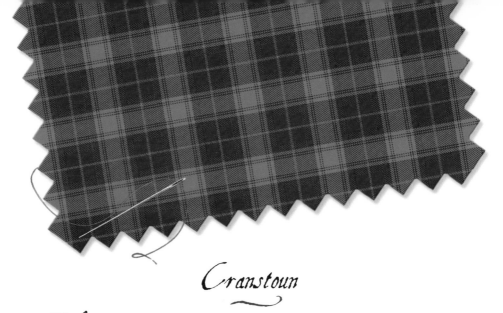

## Cranstoun

The Cranstoun seat is in the Midlothian region, the badge motif associated with a phrase translated as 'the place where cranes are seen'. Cranstouns appear as far back as the twelfth century, the first being Elfrick of Cranstoun, a Norman mercenary and a witness on a charter of William I (r. 1165–1214) for Holyrood Abbey. One Hugh de Cranstoun signed the Ragman Rolls in 1296, beginning a long tradition of Cranstoun association with the English/British government. Thomas de Cranstoun became a warden of the Marches in 1459 and Sir John Cranstoun of Morrieston ascended to the peerage in 1609.

## Crawford

**Badge:** Stag's head surmounted by a cross, with Latin motto
*Tutum te robore reddam* (I will give you safety by strength)

The Crawford family are of Norman descent, the French ancestors settling in Lanarkshire in the twelfth century, where they took the barony of Crawford. There are numerous variations on the name, including Crawfurd and Crauford, and the family developed into numerous branches spread over a wide area. The first record of the tartan was seen in the *Vestiarium Scoticum*, a history of Scottish costume by John Sobieski Stuart, published in 1842. Research shows that there was no Crawford tartan defined during the 1730s, so it was laid down at some point in the intervening years.

# Culloden

*Gaelic:* Cùil Lodair

At present, there are two dozen tartans registered under the name Culloden, such is the importance of the Culloden name in Scottish history. In April 1746, the Battle of Culloden saw the ultimate defeat of the Jacobite rebellion (and the final battle on British soil), and it has been mythologized ever since. The tartans are meant to derive from a sett worn on the battlefield by a member of Prince Charles's staff; the tartan was explained and revealed in 1893 by historian D.W. Stewart. (Stewart's son would later help found the Scottish Tartans Society.) A piece of an original Culloden coat was put on display in Kelvingrove Museum, Glasgow, in 2007.

## Cumbernauld

*Badge:* A hunting horn, with Scots motto 'Daur and Prosper'   *Gaelic:* Comar nan Allt

This tartan was created in 1987 to celebrate the achievements of the Stirlingshire town of Cumbernauld, founded in the post-war years to relieve the overcrowding of Glasgow. Its designer was Frank Gordon, a kiltmaker working out of Cumbernauld. According to the official press release, the sett was based on the MacKenzie tartan, with a variation in the colour scheme. It was noted that 'Ancient green was incorporated with modern blue, black and red to represent a new thriving community, proud of its heritage.' As with many modern tartan setts, the Cumbernauld can be worn by anyone.

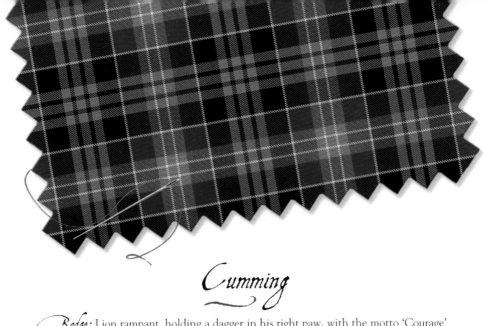

## Cumming

*Badge:* Lion rampant, holding a dagger in his right paw, with the motto 'Courage'
*Gaelic:* Cuimeineach

The French ancestry of this clan possibly reaches back to the town of Comines, from where the Norman knight Robert de Comyn took his name. Comyn came to Britain with the Norman Conquest, and was made the Earl of Northumberland in 1069. His grandson, Richard, was an attendant of King David I (r. 1124–53), and profitable marriage alliances built up the clan's authority around Atholl, Badenoch, Menteith, Montheith and Buchan. One ancestor, John Comyn, was stabbed and killed by Robert the Bruce (r. 1306–29) in 1306, resulting in a bitter war that severed Cumming power.

# Cunningham

**Badge:** Unicorn's head, with the motto 'Over fork over'  **Gaelic:** Coineagan

The Cunninghams are descended from a chief, Wernibald, who flourished during the early twelfth century when he was granted the lands of Cunninghame, Ayrshire. Alexander II (r. 1214–49) awarded the Cunninghams the lands of Kilmaurs, on account of Hervey de Cunningham's valour at the Battle of the Largs in 1263. All other Cunningham lands were confirmed by royal charter. The Cunningham motto, 'Over fork over', relates to a story that either Robert the Bruce (r. 1306–29) or Malcolm III (r. 1058–93) was hidden from enemies by a Cunningham, by forking hay over him.

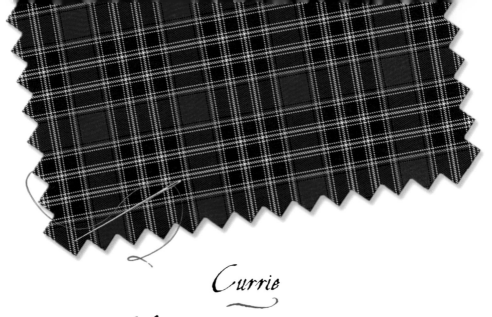

# Currie

*Gaelic:* Curaidh or MacMhuirich (Son of Murdoch)

The Currie ancestry and evolution is quite fragmented, divided between several branches of the family and different territorial lines. Branches of the Curries developed in Arran, Ayrshire, Argyll and the Isles, with some of the ancestors reaching back to the twelfth and thirteenth centuries. The founder of the Curries was the early twelfth-century bard Muireadhach Ó Dálaigh. Reflecting the desire to consolidate the traditions, in 1992, a single tartan was adopted for the entire Currie clan – previously, the design had purely been used for the Balilone and Garrachoran lines and was designed in 1822.

# Dalmeny

**Badge:** A lion holding a primrose, with Latin motto *Fide et fiducia* (Faith and trust)
**Gaelic:** Dail Mheinidh

Dalmeny is a village on the northern outskirts of Edinburgh, and the permanent settlement dates back to the early Middle Ages. The centrepiece of the village is Dalmeny Kirk, which was built in the twelfth century and stands very much untouched today, apart from a reconstructed western tower. It also has a stately home, Dalmeny House, currently the home of the Earl and Countess of Rosebery. Three district tartans are currently active, the most established of these being a version produced by the weavers Wilsons of Bannockburn in 1840.

## Dalziel

**Badge:** Dagger, with the motto 'I dare'   **Gaelic:** Dail Gheal

Dalziel (or Dalzell) was a thirteenth-century barony in Lanarkshire. Historians suggest two derivations: the first, and most likely, is from *dail gheal*, the Gaelic for 'white valley'; while the second is from the Old Scots '*Dal Zell*', which means 'I dare'. The latter cites a tale in which King Kenneth II (r. 971–95) set a challenge for someone to rescue the body of a hanged kinsman, resulting in one man stepping forward and declaring 'Dal Zell'. This tartan was produced by Wilsons of Bannockburn to celebrate the visit of King George IV (r. 1820–30) to Edinburgh in 1822.

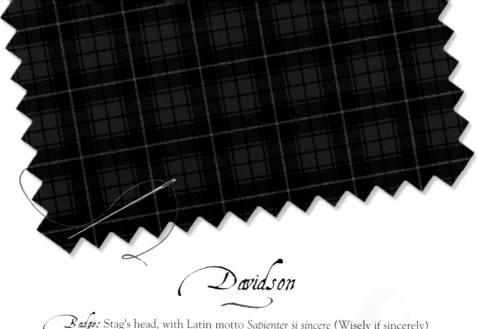

## Davidson

*Badge:* Stag's head, with Latin motto *Sapienter si sincere* (Wisely if sincerely)
*Gaelic:* MacDhaibhidh

The Davidson name begins with the nobleman David Dubh of Inverhaven, the son of Donald Dubh, who was in turn related to the Comyns (*see* page 80). As the Comyns lost much of their power in the fourteenth century, Donald made a marriage alliance with the Mackintoshes, and the Davidson clan became part of the powerful Clan Chattan confederation (*see* page 67). The alliance brought mixed blessings, including near destruction at the hands of the Camerons at Inverhaven in 1370, and further battles at North Inch of Perth (1396) and Harlaw (1411), but also expansion into Aberdeen, Perth and Dundee.

## Diana

At the time of writing, there are seven tartans in the Scottish Register of Tartans named in honour of Diana, Princess of Wales (1961–97). These were produced at various points along her royal life, from her engagement and marriage to Prince Charles in 1981 through to her untimely death in 1997. Registered designs from the early 1980s include Diana Hunting Plaid (1981) and Diana Hunting, Lady (1982), designed by Flairtex of Darvel in Ayrshire (now no longer trading). After her death, however, there was a rush of memorial tartans, including Diana Princess of Wales (Peter MacDonald, 1997) and Diana Princess of Wales Memorial (Alistair Buchan, 1997).

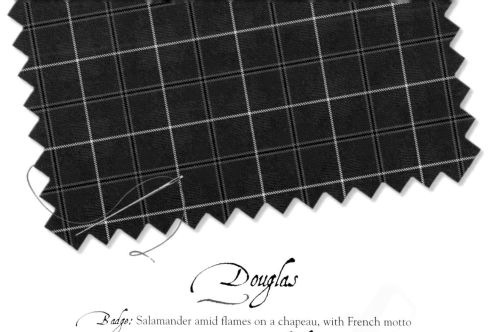

## Douglas

**Badge:** Salamander amid flames on a chapeau, with French motto *Jamais arrière* (Never behind) **Gaelic:** *Dubhghlas*

This Lanarkshire clan rose from its first recorded appearance in the twelfth century to become one of the most potent of all Scottish clans. *Dubhghlas*, translated as 'dark water', is possibly a reference to a stream running through a Douglas estate. William de Douglas is the first name to appear in the clan's history, and his six sons went on to establish powerful lines of influence in British politics and land ownership. Although the Douglases suffered several family splits, their power ensured that they spawned numerous dukes, earls and marquises.

## Drummond

**Badge:** Goshawk, with the motto 'Gang warily' **Gaelic:** Druimeineach

Named after the Drymen estates in Stirlingshire, this clan traces its progenitors back to the eleventh century and Hungarian followers of Prince Edgar (the great nephew of Edward the Confessor). Its first chief was Malcolm Beag in the thirteenth century, and one of his line, Sir Malcolm de Drummond, was famously granted Perthshire landholdings by Robert the Bruce (r. 1306–29) after his distribution of caltrops (early antipersonnel weapons such as metal sandburrs) stopped the English cavalry charging at the Battle of Bannockburn. There are currently a total of 18 tartans associated with the Drummond clan.

## Dunbar

**Badge:** Plumed horse's head, with Latin motto *Candoris praemium honos*
(Honour is the reward of integrity)  **Gaelic:** *Dùn Barra*

Two patterns of Dunbar tartan seem to have been in existence by the mid-1800s: a family sett and a district/family sett woven by Wilsons of Bannockburn in 1850. The distinction reflects the fact that the Dunbar name is both familial and geographical, related to the East Lothian port of Dunbar. Crinan, father of King Duncan I (*r.* 1034–40), marks the beginning of the Dunbar line, as his son Gospatric was granted the Dunbar lands by Malcolm III (*r.* 1058–93) in 1072. The port later became a royal burgh, in 1369.

## Dunblane

*Badge:* Crown and a hand on one side, with flames and Latin motto *Renovate animus veritate* (Renew your courage with truth)   *Gaelic:* Dùn Bhlàthain

The small town of Dunblane to the north of Stirling has one main tartan, associated with both the family and territory. It is based on a design seen in a portrait of Peregrine, 2nd Viscount Dunblane, displayed at Hornby Castle in Yorkshire. Peregrine died in 1729, so the tartan is at least eighteenth century in origin, and probably earlier. The sett largely fell out of use until the rejuvenating effects of George IV's visit to Edinburgh in 1822, when the tartan was brought out for the occasion, along with many other traditional setts.

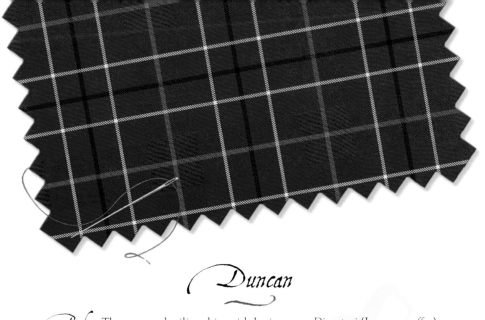

## Duncan

**Badge:** Three-masted sailing ship, with Latin motto *Disce pati* (Learn to suffer)
**Gaelic:** Donnchadh

The Duncan name was originally, and still is, a forename, as we see in the case of two early Scottish kings. As a family, the Duncans were originally a sept of the Robertsons – the Robertsons had the title clan *Clann Donnchaidh*, meaning children of Duncan, until they formally adopted the Robertson name in the mid-1400s. The Duncans' robustly named progenitor was Donnchadh Reamhar (Duncan the Fat), 5th Lord of Glenorchie, who made a signal contribution to the Scottish victory at Bannockburn, and the Duncans went on to produce several great military leaders.

## Dundas

**Badge:** Lion's head and young oak, with French motto *Essayez* (Try)   **Gaelic:** Dùn Deas

Records of the Dundas clan start during the reign of William I (r. 1165–1214), during which there is an account of one Serle of Dundas holding lands in West Lothian. One of the great Dundas figures was undoubtedly Henry Dundas (1742–1811), a lawyer, politician and the 1st Viscount Melville. Dundas managed to restore, through the British parliament, many of the estates forfeited after the Jacobite rebellion. He also served as the British War Secretary and First Lord of the Admiralty, but was impeached and removed from office in 1806.

## Dundee

*Badge:* Three lilies presented in a pot, with Latin motto *Prudentia et candore*
(With prudence and purity)   *Gaelic:* Dùn Dèagh

Dundee illustrates how district tartans can be created to fit in with the many aspects of a city. The 'core' Dundee tartan is based upon a tartan jacket said to have been worn by Prince Charles Edward Stuart (1720–88) at the Battle of Culloden in 1746, the pattern becoming more established through its production by Wilsons of Bannockburn, the famous weaving company established in *c.* 1770. Today, however, there are tartans associated with Dundee District Council, Dundee United Football Club and Dundee University, to name three of 12 Dundee setts.

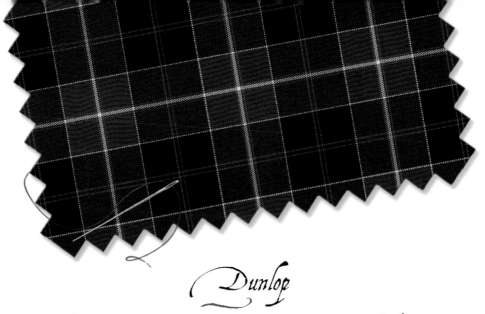

## Dunlop

*Badge:* Hand holding a dagger, with Latin motto *Merito* (By merit)   *Gaelic:* Dùn Lùib

Today, the Dunlop name is most famously associated with the inventor John Boyd Dunlop (1840–1921), whose creation of the pneumatic tyre revolutionized transport. The origins of the name lie with the Ayrshire village of Dunlop near Kilmarnock, and Dunlop ancestors appear as signatories on the Ragman Rolls in 1296. A family tartan does not seem to have been established until well into the twentieth century, when Richard Dunlop of Washington DC, the second President of the Dunlop Family Clan Society, oversaw a finalized design in 1982.

## Dunoon

*Badge:* Three-towered castle surmounted by a galley, with the motto 'Forward'
*Gaelic:* Dùn Omhain

Dunoon is a resort town on the coast of Argyll by the Firth of Clyde. Its history reaches back to the eleventh century, when Dunoon Castle was built and served as a critical coastal strongpoint for several hundred years. Much of the town's development took place in the nineteenth and twentieth centuries, including the construction of Castle House and Dunoon Pier. The tartan is also a twentieth-century invention. It was designed by Harry Bayne and registered on 1 January 1935, being classified as a corporate tartan because of its use by the Glasgow Irish Pipe Band.

## Durie

The Durie name derives from the village near Scoonie in Fife, with modern members of the Durie clan claiming an ancestry as far back as the twelfth century. Certainly the name Durie appears in official documents from 1238, although the clan seems to have been without an official head for many centuries. This situation was only rectified in the 1980s, when Lieutenant Colonel Raymond Durie took the role as clan chief. A tartan was created in response to this event, the design, by Harry Kindley for Kinlock Anderson Ltd, being registered on 1 January 1994.

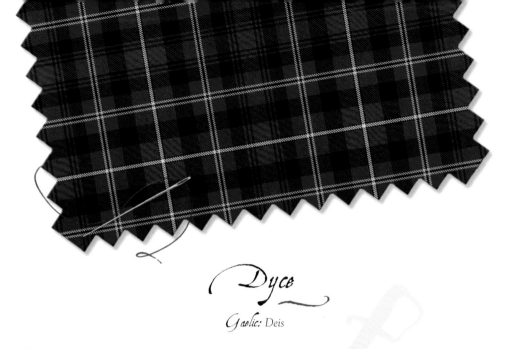

## Dyce

*Gaelic:* Deis

Records from 1467 list one John de Diss as a burgess of Aberdeen, showing that the Dyce clan was established in this region by the fifteenth century. (There are several other variant spellings of the name, including Dyos, Dyess and Dias.) Since this time, several Dyces have left their mark on cultural and public affairs. They include the influential nineteenth-century editor Alexander Dyce (1798–1869) and the artist William Dyce (1806–64), who was an early pioneer of the Pre-Raphaelite movement. There are three Dyce tartans currently registered, the earliest version being created in 1906, based on an earlier pattern displayed in the 1880 publication *Clans Originaux.*

# Edinburgh

*Badge:* Three-towered castle, with Latin motto *Nisi dominus frustra*
(It is vanity, unless the Lord wills it)   *Gaelic: Dùn Éideann* (Edwin's burgh)

Being the great capital city of Scotland, Edinburgh has naturally generated a large number of tartans associated with its institutions, events and history. The Scottish Register of Tartans lists 30 varieties of Edinburgh tartan, ranging from rich and intense tapestries of reds, greens, whites and blues, through to muted panels of greys and purples. Particularly interesting are a special design created for the 50th anniversary of the Edinburgh Military Tattoo in 2000, a corporate sett designed for Edinburgh Napier University and a pattern created in the 1950s for the Duke of Edinburgh.

## Elliot

**Badge:** Armoured fist holding a sword, with Latin motto *Braviter et recte* (Bravely and justly)

The Elliot tartan stands out from most others, being a vivid combination of maroon and blue. It was recorded in 1880 in the *Clans Originaux*, but references to the Elliots date back to the time of Robert the Bruce (*r.* 1306–29). There are also records of Robert Elliot of Redheugh, the 10th clan chief, dating to 1476. The Elliot name later became associated with Britain's colonial governance. Sir Gilbert Elliot of Minto (1751–1814) was the Governor General of India, while the 4th earl, also Gilbert (1845–1914), was the Governor General of Canada and Viceroy of India.

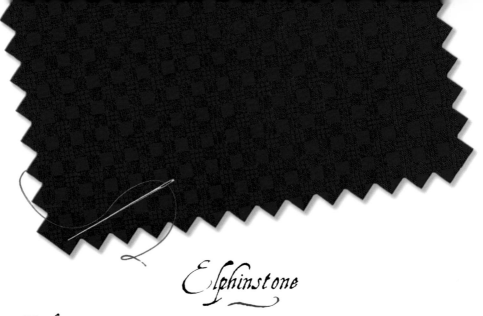

## Elphinstone

*Badge:* Lady holding a tower and laurel branch, with the motto *Cause causit* (Cause causes)

The Elphinstones are an East Lothian family connected with the village of the same name, near Tranent. Early leaders of the Elphinstones include Sir Henry Elphinstone, created a baron in 1509 and killed at the Battle of Flodden in 1513, and William Elphinstone (1431–1514), the Bishop of Aberdeen and the Lord Chancellor. During the nineteenth century, many Elphinstones served in the British possessions in India and Afghanistan. Major General William George Elphinstone (1782–1842) famously led the British garrison at Kabul to disaster in 1842 – he died a prisoner of the Afghans.

## Erskine

**Badge:** Demi-lion rampant, with Latin motto *Decori decus addit avito*
(He adds honour to his ancestors) **Gaelic:** *Arasgain*

The traditional Erskine lands are in Renfrewshire, and there is a record of one Henry of Erskine dating back to the thirteenth century. The Erskines grew to be a significant clan in Scotland, partly through marrying into powerful families such as the Bruce and Stewart clans. Further acquisitions of power came with the earldom of Kellie in 1619. Yet the Erskines later lost significant land and power after their backing of the 1715 Jacobite Rising.

## Falkirk

*Badge:* Falkirk church, with shield and crossed claymores, with Scots motto
'Touch ane, touch a'' (Touch one, touch all) *Gaelic:* An Eaglais Bhreac

Falkirk in Stirlingshire has a critical place in Scottish history. In 1298, William Wallace (d. 1305) was defeated here by the forces of Edward I (r. 1272–1307), and, in 1746, another battle saw the crushing of the Jacobite rebellion under Bonnie Prince Charlie (1720–88). Both events had deep effects on the course of Scottish history and politics. The Falkirk tartan is based upon a piece of cloth found stuffed in a pot (along with two thousand silver coins) dating back to *c.* 250 AD, during the period of Roman occupation.

# Farquharson

**Badge:** Demi-lion rampant holding a sword, with Latin motto *Fide et fortitudine* (By faith and fortitude) **Gaelic:** MacFhearchair

The progenitor of the Farquharson clan was Farquhar, the son of Alexander Ciar (Shaw) of Rothiemurchus. Farquhar, born in the fourteenth century, took over lands taken from the Comyns during the reign of Robert the Bruce (r. 1306–29). (The Farquharsons are part of the Clan Chattan.) During the Anglo-Scottish Wars, Finlay Mór, Farquhar's grandson, was a standard bearer for the king at the Battle of Pinkie in 1547, where he was killed. Finlay is often seen as the true beginning of the Farquharsons, being titled the 1st Farquharson Lord of Invercauld.

## Ferguson

*Badge:* Crowned lion rampant and crown, with Gaelic motto
*Clann Fhearghais gu bràth* (Clan Fergus for ever)  *Gaelic:* MacFhearghais

The Fergusons ('Fergusson' is another common spelling) are not a single unified clan, but a collection of families distributed across Scotland and sharing a common name. At the height of their power in the Renaissance, the Fergusons had power bases in Argyll, Perthshire, Aberdeenshire, Galloway and Carrick, although, today, Argyllshire and Perthshire have the main concentrations of Ferguson landholdings. Fergusons claim their descent through various historical figures, such as Fergus MacFergus, who acquired lands in Ayrshire from Robert the Bruce (r. 1306–29) and gave rise to the Kilkerran family of Fergusons.

# Ferguson of Balquhidder

*Gaelic:* MacFhearghais Bhoth Phuidir

The Fergusons are, naturally enough, associated with the district of Balquhidder in Perthshire. Actually, these lands have been historically connected to the MacLaren clan, although the MacLarens lost these lands in the nineteenth century, at which point the Fergusons stepped in. In addition to the Fergusons and the MacLarens, Balquhidder is also associated with Rob Roy and this is where the outlaw is buried. The most senior branch of the Fergusons is the Fergusons of Kilkerran, Ayrshire, to which the Balquhidder family is related. There are three Ferguson of Balquhidder tartans, dating from an example registered in 1831 and designed by J. Logan, through to a sample created, or at least registered, between 1930 and 1950.

## Fiddes

Records of Fiddes tartans date back to the eighteenth century, the earliest recorded example being designed by Wilsons of Bannockburn in 1790. The threadcount (the number of threads per linear inch) of this early tartan, however, is unclear and, in 1975, another sett was issued that was meant to give the correct design. Today, there are six Fiddes tartans registered, including a personal version registered in 2007 for a Jason Dalley of Wiltshire. The Fiddes name related to the barony of Fiddes in Kincardineshire, which is no longer in existence. Early versions of the name include Fotheis and Fothes, and are seen in local documents dating back to the thirteenth century. A number of later clan members pursued careers as churchmen, including Sir William Fudes who became Chancellor of Caithness in 1524.

# Fletcher

**Badge:** Demi-lion holding a cross, with Latin motto *Libertate extincta nula virtus* (Where liberty is dead, there is no valour)  **Gaelic:** *Mac an Fhleisdeir*

The Fletcher clan developed in Perthshire and Argyllshire, the name deriving from the French term *fléchier* ('maker of arrows'). True to their name, the earliest Fletchers were known as arrowmakers, the Fletchers of Argyll serving the Stewarts and Campbells, while the Fletchers of Perthshire worked for the MacGregors. Over time, the Fletchers' relationship with the other clans was often fraught; although they acquired lands in Glenlochry in the sixteenth century, they were eventually driven out by the Campbells. Famous Fletchers include Andrew Fletcher (1653–1716), who fought against the 1707 Act of Union.

# Forbes

**Badge:** Stag's head, with the motto 'Grace me guide'  **Gaelic:** Foirbeis

The traditional Forbes territories are along the River Don in Aberdeenshire, and legend has it that the ancestral lands were first claimed by a Celtic warrior named Ochanachar who, having killed a wild boar that was threatening locals, then claimed the territory for himself. More substantial evidence points to John of Forbes during the reign of William I (r. 1165–1214), then Duncan of Forbes in the thirteenth century, who was officially granted the Forbes lands by Alexander III. The clan seat is the great Castle Forbes, built by the seventeenth-century Lord Forbes in 1815.

## Forrester

*Gaelic:* Mac an Fhòrsair

A Lowland clan originating around Dunipace, Stirlingshire, the Forresters are actually an armigerous clan, meaning that, because they have no chief officially recognized by the Lord Lyon King of Arms, they have no particular clan rights under Scottish law. Although a Dunipace landowner named Marnin Forrester is recorded c. 1200, the true progenitor is regarded as Sir Adam Forrester (d. 1405), a fourteenth-century merchant who rose to become Provost of Edinburgh, Keeper of the Great Seal of Scotland and Deputy Chamberlain of Scotland. From the fourteenth to the seventeenth century, the Forresters frequently battled against the English. They supported the royalist cause during the Civil War.

# Forsyth

*Badge:* Griffin sergeant and armed, with Latin motto *Instaurator ruinae* (A restorer of ruins)

*Gaelic:* Fear Sithe (Man of peace)

Although the Forsyth name is held by many to derive from the Gaelic *fear sithe* ('man of peace'), it may have a Norman ancestry – a family named de Fronsoc settled in Britain during the thirteenth century in the area around Edinburgh. The Forsyth name (as Robert de Fauside) is on the Ragman Rolls of 1296, although his son Osbert fought for Robert the Bruce (r. 1306–29) and was granted the territories of Sauchie, Stirling. For some 300 years from the seventeenth century, the clan chief was not officially recognized, a situation rectified in 1980.

## Fraser

*Badge:* Buck's head, with French motto *Je suis prest* (I am ready) *Gaelic:* Friseal

The Frasers are one of the great clans of Scotland, descended from Normans who settled in Tweeddale during the eleventh century. Two main kindreds evolved – the Lovat Frasers of Inverness-shire and the Philorth Frasers of Aberdeenshire. Both sides of the clan have produced vivid historical characters, including the 8th Lord of Philorth, Alexander (*c.* 1537–1623), responsible for founding the port of Fraserburgh, and Simon (*c.* 1667–1747), 11th Lord of Lovat, the last person to be beheaded in the Tower of London, on 9 April 1747, following the failed Jacobite rebellion.

## Galbraith

*Badge:* Muzzled boar's head, with Latin motto *Ab obice suavior* (Smoother for the difficulties)

*Gaelic:* Mac a' Bhreatannaich (Son of the Britishman)

The intriguing Gaelic name of the Galbraith clan refers to the kingdom of Britons established around Strathclyde from the sixth century AD, which is believed to have provided the Galbraiths with their founder in the form of one Gilchrist Bretnach. The family rose to take high official position – Sir William Galbraith was co-Regent of Scotland in 1255 under Alexander III (r. 1249–86), but, during the early Renaissance, the power base collapsed and all lands were lost. Because the downfall brought the line of chiefs to an end, the Galbraiths are now classified as an armigerous clan (*see* page 108).

## Galloway

*Badge:* Nesting pelican, feeding young with own blood, with Latin motto *Virescit vulnere virtus* (Courage is strengthened by a wound)  *Gaelic:* Gall-Ghàidhealaibh (Land of foreigners)

The Galloway region, in the far south-west of Scotland, was settled in ancient times, and the Romans of the first century AD named the inhabitants the Novantae. Irish influence was strong over the region (hence its Gaelic name), becoming part of the English kingdom of Bernicia during the seventh century, which was in turn displaced by the Vikings during the ninth and tenth centuries. The region subsequently shifted its loyalties between England and Scotland. Nine tartans are currently registered under the Galloway name, most being twentieth-century creations.

## Gillies

*Gaelic:* MacGilllosa (Son of the servant of Jesus)

The religious meaning of the Gaelic word for Gillies suggests that the family may have derived from churchmen. These ecclesiastical connections are reinforced by the fact that the Gillies are treated as a sept of the MacPhersons, whose Gaelic name is translated as 'son of the parson'. Associated with the Hebrides and Badenoch, the Gillies name is an old one, seen on a royal charter in 1128. There are currently seven Gillies tartans registered, including a royal version registered in the first half of the twentieth century and known as the Balmoral Gillies.

# Glasgow

**Badge:** Bell, tree, bird, salmon and ring, with the motto 'Let Glasgow flourish'
**Gaelic:** Glaschu (The dear green place)

Scotland's second city originated as a small fishing village which, during the 600s, acquired a church that grew into the cathedral, making Glasgow a place of worship and ecclesiastical authority. Glasgow's growth accelerated from the seventeenth century, when the foundation of British colonies in North America led to a major increase in the city's trade, particularly in tobacco. Although the city's subsequent industrialization was a curse as much as a blessing, during the twentieth century, Glasgow retained its place as a centre of international trade. Nineteen district, corporate and fashion tartans are currently associated with Glasgow.

## Gordon

*Badge:* Buck's head, with Lowland Scots motto *Bydand* (Remaining)  *Gaelic:* Gòrdan

Gordon ancestors, Norman settlers, put down roots in a parish near Edinburgh in the twelfth century. A significant expansion in power took place in the early 1300s, when Sir Adam of Gordon, a comrade of Robert the Bruce (*r.* 1306–29), was given the lordship of Strathbogie for undertaking a diplomatic mission to the pope in 1320. Such was the power of the Gordon clan by the sixteenth and seventeenth centuries that its chief was known as the 'cock o' the north'. The Gordons are famous for the Gordon Highlanders regiment, founded in 1794.

## Gordon of Abergeldie

*Gaelic:* Gòrdanach Obar Gheallaidh

The power and size of the Gordon clan meant that the family produced many different branches, each with its own local area of influence. At times, this meant that the Gordons developed internal split loyalties. During the Jacobite rebellions of 1715 and 1745, for example, Gordons could be found on both the rebel and the government sides. The Gordons of Abergeldie take their name from Abergeldie Castle on the River Dee, a Gordon residence. This particular tartan is taken from a portrait of Rachael Gordon of Abergeldie, painted in 1723. It is one of more than 30 Gordon tartans, including that of the 92nd Gordon Highlanders and various local setts.

## Gordonstoun

This famous and prestigious independent school in Moray is known for educating three generations of the royal family. It was originally known as the House of Plewlands but, in 1638, it was purchased by Sir Robert Gordon (1580–1661). The building's transformation into a leading school began when it was purchased by German educationalist Kurt Hahn (1886–1974), who created the modern institution in the 1930s (Hahn had fled Germany to escape the effects of the rising Nazi regime). There are four tartans associated with Gordonstoun according to the Scottish Register of Tartans, all designed during the 1950s and 1960s by designers such as Gordon Stewart and Gilbert Duncan Macleod Bullard.

## Gow

*Badge:* Thistle, with Latin motto *Juncta arma decori* (Arms united for glory)
*Gaelic:* Mac a' Ghobhainn (Son of the smith)

The Gow name has its origins in Inverness-shire and Perthshire. Its origin lies in the Gaelic *Gobha*, which means a blacksmith, and hence the title was linked with many clans in Scotland, although the main Highland family of Gows is regarded as being a sept of the MacPherson clan. A distinct branch of the Gows is the clan MacGowan, originally from areas such as Stirling, Dumfries, Fife and Glasgow. There are several varieties of Gow tartan, one based on a 1780 portrait of the famous fiddler Niel Gow (1727–1807) by Sir Henry Raeburn (1717–1807).

# Graham of Menteith

*Badge:* Falcon proper, with French motto *N'oubliez* (Do not forget)
*Gaelic: Greumach Thèadhaich*

Another of the great Scottish clans, the Grahams are by tradition descended from Greme, a Pictish chief who fought the Romans during the second century AD, although Anglo-Norman ancestry is much more likely. The first definable ancestor is William of Graham who, as part of King David I's retinue, was granted the lands of Abercorn and Dalkeith in 1127. The tartan here is of the Menteith branch of the Grahams, created when James I (r. 1406–37) bestowed the title Earl of Menteith upon the former Earl of Strathearn Malise Graham (1406–90).

# Graham of Montrose

*Badge:* Eagle attacking a stork, with French motto *N'oubliez* (Do not forget)
*Gaelic:* Greumach Mhon Rois

Notable Grahams are Sir John Graham of Dundaff, known as the 'right hand' of William Wallace (he died at Falkirk in 1298) and John Graham of Claverhouse, who led the Jacobites in support of James VII (r. 1685–88) and died after being wounded at the Battle of Killiecrankie in 1689. The Montrose line has produced some impressive figures, such as James Graham (1615–50), the 5th Earl and 1st Marquis of Montrose. Montrose became one of Charles I's leading generals during the English Civil War, but was finally captured and executed in Edinburgh in May 1650.

## Grampian

*Badge:* Cross-crosslet on a saltire cross   *Gaelic:* Am Monadh

Grampian is used to define a territory consisting of large parts of north-east Scotland, and today encompassing the unitary council areas of Moray, Aberdeenshire and the City of Aberdeen. It includes some mountainous areas, and takes its name from a corruption of Mons Graupius, a battle fought in 83 or 84 AD between the Romans and the Caledonian Confederacy. (The Romans won.) The main district tartan was registered in 1995, its colours reflecting those of the Grampian mountains, while there are also corporate tartans for the Grampian Police and Grampian Television.

# Grant

*Badge:* Burning mountain, with the motto 'Stand fast'   *Gaelic:* Grannd

Although the derivation of the Grant name is unclear (the French *grand* – 'great' – is probable), there is no doubting the power that the Grants achieved. The clan began its rise to prominence in the Highlands during the twelfth and thirteenth centuries, becoming sheriffs of Inverness in the 1260s, and Sir Duncan le Grant acquiring the barony of Freuchie in 1494. While the Grants fought for the royalists during the English Civil War, during the Jacobite rebellion, the clan had divided loyalties and even fought with each other. Today, there are numerous different lines of Grants.

## Grant of Monymusk

*Badge:* Sun shining on a tree trunk, with Latin motto *Te favente virebo*
(Under your favour, I will flourish)  *Gaelic:* Granndach Mhòine Muiseig

The Grants of Monymusk grew from the village of Monymusk in Aberdeenshire, the site of a sixth-century Augustinian priory. While the primary tartan for the Grant clan is known as the 1860 sett, there are numerous variant tartans designed for the different family lines. At the time of writing, there are 24 tartans registered under the Grant name, including the Grant of Monymusk tartan seen here, which dates back to the early nineteenth century. Others include the Grant of Achnarrow, Grant of Ballindalloch and Grant of Rothiemurchus.

# Gunn

*Badge:* Right hand holding a broadsword, with Latin motto
*Aut pax aut bellum* (Either peace or war)   *Gaelic:* Guinne

A story goes that Gunni, a Norse chief (son of Olaf the Black), came over to Scotland in the twelfth century, and his wife Ragnor took possession of territories around Caithness during the same century. A more supportable account is that the Gunns emerged from a Pictish tribe that inhabited the same area. True to their motto, the Gunns were a fiery and belligerent clan, raiding the territory of other clans and, in later history, providing a good number of senior military leaders.

# Guthrie

**Badge:** Right hand holding a sword, with Latin motto *Sto pro veritate* (I stand for truth)

The Guthrie name may have Norse origins and be derived from a prince Guthrum (d. 880), although it is more tangibly linked to the village of Gutherie and the lands of Gutherin in Tayside. An early reference comes from 1299, when the squire of Guthrie travelled to France to persuade William Wallace (d. 1305) to return to Scotland to battle the incursions of King Edward I (r. 1272–1307). Another prominent Guthrie was Sir David Guthrie (1435–1500), the Sheriff of Forfar, who was appointed Lord Chief Justice of Scotland in 1473.

## Haig

**Badge:** Group of rocks, with the motto 'Tyde what may'

The Haigs are descended from the Norman noble Petrus de Haga. De Haga acquired the original Haig lands of Bemersyde in Roxburghshire during the twelfth century. These lands stayed in the family until the mid-nineteenth century, during which time the Haigs served Scotland against the English in the various wars for independence. History's most famous Haig was Field Marshal Sir Douglas Haig (1861–1928), commander of British forces during the First World War, who in 1919 was made the 1st Earl Haig for his services to Britain, although those services are today seen as highly controversial.

## Hamilton

*Badge:* Oak tree on a ducal coronet, with the motto 'Through'  *Gaelic:* Hamalton

The roots of the Hamilton clan lie in the southern English village of Hambledon, Hampshire. A Norman knight of the area, Walter Fitz Gilbert of Hambledon, settled in Scotland during the thirteenth century in Renfrewshire, and became the governor of Bothwell Castle and the clan progenitor. Over time, the Hamiltons became an extremely powerful clan, with deep marital and official connections with the Scottish royalty. There are seven tartans associated with the Hamiltons. The first recorded example was seen in the *Vestiarium Scoticum* of 1842, although this sett was based on a forged manuscript.

## Hannay

**Badge:** Cross-crosslet fitchee issuing from a crescent, with Latin motto *Per ardua ad alta* (Through difficulties to the heights) **Gaelic:** Ò hAnnaidh

With their territorial origins in Galloway in south-western Scotland, the Hannay clan is first recorded in that most useful of sources, the Ragman Rolls of 1296, although their origins predate this time and relate to earlier Celtic settlements in the area. The Hannays acquired lands around Sorbie during the thirteenth and fourteenth centuries but, during the seventeenth century, a feud with the Murrays of Broughton ruined the Sorbie line, and consequently the Hannays of Kirkdale rose to control the clan. The black and white Hannay tartan is typical of many Lowland clans.

## Hardie

The Hardie surname is likely to be of Norman origin, deriving from the Old French word *hardi*, meaning 'bold' or 'daring'. A Lanarkshire landowner called William Hardy appears on the Ragman Rolls in 1296 and, from the fifteenth century onwards, the Hardie name is frequent in local government and judicial records. (Note that there are many variant spellings, including Hardy, Hardey and Hardee.) One particularly famous Hardie from history is James Keir Hardie (1856–1915). Hardie was a former miner and passionate socialist and, in 1892, he became the first independent labour candidate to win a seat in the British parliament. He went on to become a founder of the Labour Party.

# Hay

*Badge:* Falcon with outstretched wings, with Latin motto *Serva jugum* (Save the yoke)
*Gaelic:* Mac Garaidh

The falcon on the Hay badge relates to one particular origin tradition. During the battle of Luncarty (c. 971) against the Danes, Kenneth III (r. 997–1005) was supposed to have ordered the release of a falcon and promised that whoever rose as the hero of the battle would possess the lands as far as the bird flew. In reality, the Hays are likely to be another Norman import and, in 1178, there is a reference to a William de Haye, serving as cupbearer to Malcolm IV (r. 1153–65) and possessing lands around Errol in Perthshire.

# Hebridean

*Gaelic:* Eileanach

The Hebrides consist of more than 130 islands (although not all are or have been inhabited), and records seem to suggest that each island could have its own sett of tartan, with variations within communities. Such diversity is not uncommon among peoples who have made much of their living from fishing, and pattern distinctions were often a way of identifying those who had drowned at sea. Two of the oldest Hebridean tartans in existence date back to the early eighteenth century and appear to be connected to specific families, but most of the patterns existing today are fashion versions produced for the tourist market.

# Henderson

**Badge:** Hand holding a star surmounted by a crescent, with Latin motto *Sola virtus nobilitat* (Valour alone gives nobility)  **Gaelic:** MacEanraig

The Henderson clan is scattered at various different points across Scotland, hence there is a variety of origin myths and traditions, changing according to the location. A unifying idea, although one that is largely historically discredited, is that the Hendersons are descended from an eighth-century Caledonian prince named Eanraig Mór mac Rìgh Neachtan, or 'Big Henry'. (Note also that the Gaelic of the Henderson name is often translated as MacKendrick.) The Hendersons became a clan of respectable power by the end of the Middle Ages, with strongholds in Caithness, Glencoe, the Shetland Islands and Fife.

*Herd*

Tartans can be created for many reasons, not only acting as a representative pattern of a clan or family. The Scottish Register of Tartans places tartans according to their categories of purpose, which include Clan/Family, Name, Fashion, Royal, District, Military and Corporate, each describing the intended context of the sett. The Herd tartan is a 'Name' tartan, which is described as 'A tartan intended to be worn by anyone of that name, or a personal tartan for a particular person and his/her immediate family.' In this case, the tartan was registered in 1978 as 'Woven for the wedding of William Hurd to Heather Petit' and is based upon the similar Gunn tartan.

## Holyrood

Located at the bottom of the Royal Mile in Edinburgh, the Palace of Holyroodhouse was originally a monastery, founded in 1128, but became the official royal residence in Scotland from the fifteenth century. The palace has witnessed the high drama of Scottish politics, including balls hosted by Bonnie Prince Charlie (1720–88) and the murder of David Rizzio (c. 1533–66), the confidant of Mary, Queen of Scots (1542–87). The first 'Holyrood' tartan was designed by Alistair Buchan of Lochcarron of Scotland to commemorate the Silver Jubilee of Queen Elizabeth II in 1977, and Buchan followed up with another tartan to commemorate her Golden Jubilee in 2002.

## Home

**Badge:** Lion's head on a cap of maintenance, with the motto 'A home, a home, a home'

**Gaelic:** Uamh (Cave)

The Home/Hume name ('Home' is also pronounced as 'Hume') grew out of Berwickshire, the first recorded instance being Aldan de Home in 1190. The power and status of the clan readily increased, with strong connections into the royal households. In more modern times, the name Hume has become particularly well known. The Scottish philosopher, historian and economist David Hume (1711–76) became infamous for his work on moral philosophy and especially for his attacks on the Christian religion. Sir Alex Douglas Home (1903–95) was the British Prime Minister from 1963–64.

## Hope

The Hope border clan was established in Peebleshire as early as the thirteenth century – there is the signature of one John de Hop on the Ragman Rolls in 1296. In the sixteenth century, a John of Hope settled in Edinburgh, having arrived from France as part of the retinue of Madeleine de Valois (1520–37), who married James V (r. 1513–42). He established the main line of the clan, which would be influential in Scottish politics and governance. Sir Thomas Hope (c. 1580–1646), for example, helped draft the 1638 National Covenant, an affirmation of commitment to the Scottish Presbyterian tradition against English religious impositions.

## Houston

### Gaelic: Ùisdean

*E*arly members of the Houston clan were settled in Renfrewshire by the late twelfth century – settlement records of a man named Ùisdean (Gaelic equivalent of Hugh) date back to 1190. There is some evidence to suggest that a Houston was given the rank of knight and an estate in Renfrewshire during the twelfth century. The Houston name has become most distinguished by its American associations. Houston migration to North America began around the seventeenth century. The city of Houston, Texas, was named after Sam Houston (1793–1863), a general and 1st and 3rd President of the Republic of Texas.

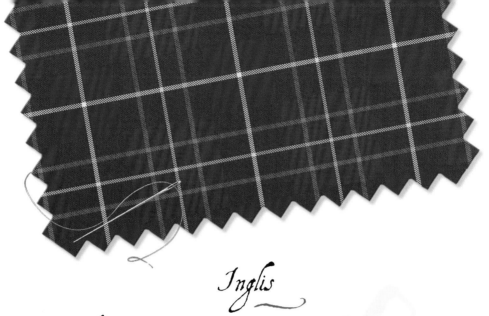

# Inglis

**Badge:** Demi-lion holding a mullet, with Latin motto *Recte faciendo securus*
(Sure in doing the right thing)

As the name suggests, the Inglis family name has its origin south of the Scottish border. It is likely that the ancestors of the Inglis family were English men and women driven north by the Norman invasion in 1066. The Inglis tartan is heavily related to the Macintyre tartan, the main distinction being that the yellow line on the Inglis tartan is green on the Macintyre sett. The Scottish Register of Tartans notes that 'There is also an ancient Inglis version of the tartan which has much lighter colour tones.'

## Innes

*Badge:* Boar's head, with the motto *Be traist* (Be faithful)    *Gaelic:* Aonghas

The Innes name has its ancestral home in Morayshire. In 1160, the Flemish lord and mercenary Berowald was granted the barony of Innes. The barony became a surname with Berowald's grandson, Walter, in 1226, when Alexander II (r. 1214–49) confirmed the lands by charter, and the family acquired substantial landholdings and developed closer relationships with Scottish and later British royalty. Innes descendants held roles such as the armour-bearer to James III (r. 1460–88). In 1812, Sir James Innes also acquired the title of 5th Duke of Roxburghe (1736–1823).

## Inverness

Gaelic: Inbhir Nis

Sometimes referred to as the 'Capital of the Highlands', the city of Inverness dates back to at least the early Middle Ages, when it was the centre of the Pictish kingdom. During the sixth century, St Columba (521–597) visited the kingdom to convert King Brude (c. 555–84) to Christianity, and Inverness was made a royal burgh in 1158 by King Malcolm IV (r. 1153–65). Although it grew throughout its history, Inverness was only granted city status in 2000. There are many different varieties of Inverness tartan, although the principal district tartan is dated to the early nineteenth century.

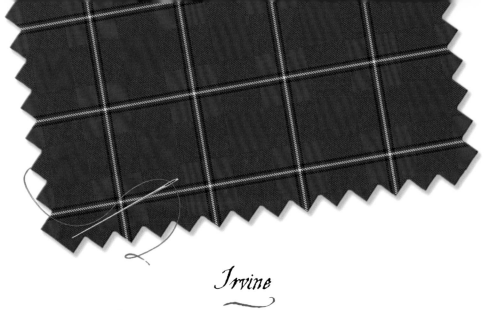

## Irvine

*Badge:* Sheath of holly, with Latin motto *Sub sole sub umbra virens*
(Flourishing in sunshine and shade)   *Gaelic:* Irbhinn

Duncan Eryvine, a tenth-century Celtic nobleman, is the likely candidate for the Irvine progenitor – the parishes of Irving in Dumfriesshire and Irvine in Ayrshire are other possible sources of the name, or the settlements founded by the Eryvine ancestors. Over the next three centuries, however, the clan put down its main roots in Dumfriesshire. An important step in their growth of power occurred during the time of William Wallace (d. 1305), when one of his retinue, William of Irvine, was granted the Forest of Drum in Aberdeenshire, where the family castle was built.

## Jacobite

**Badge:** A white rose  **Gaelic:** Seumasach

The word 'Jacobite' has a strong resonance in Scottish history. It refers to supporters of the restoration of the Stuart royal dynasty after 1688, when James VII and II (r. 1685–88) was deposed, leaving the way open for the accession of William of Orange (r. 1689–1702). Over the next century, the Jacobites fought for their cause, with major rebellions in 1715 and 1745–46. Sashes of tartan were often worn by the rebels, leading to the British government banning tartan from 1747 to 1782. The current Jacobite tartan has an ancestry stretching back into the early eighteenth century. It can be worn by anyone, regardless of clan, but has especially strong connections with the Highlands.

## Jardine

*Badge:* Six-pointed spur rowel, with Latin motto *Cave adsum* (Look out, I am here)

The Jardine name is a Norman import, derived from the French word *jardin* (garden). First reference to a Jardine comes in 1153, when one Wmfredus de Jardine appears as a witness to charters for the abbeys of Kelso and Arbroath, although the family is believed to have arrived in Britain in 1066. From Kendal they moved to Lanarkshire and then Dumfriesshire. Notable Jardines include the surgeon William Jardine (1784–1843), known for his part in starting the Opium War (1839–42) and the Scottish naturalist Sir William Jardine (1800–74), 7th Baronet of Applegirth, Dumfriesshire.

# Johnston

Badge: Phoenix rising from flames, with Latin motto *Vive ut postia vivas*
(Live that you may live hereafter) Gaelic: MacIain

In 1174, John of Johnstone was granted lands in Annandale that he called 'John's toun'. His son Gilbert took the place name as a surname and gradually the Johnstons grew to be one of the most powerful of the Border clans. Johnstons are often seen on the field of battle. James Johnston (1625–72), Lord of Lochwood, fought for Charles I (1625–49) during the Civil War, but was captured at Philiphaugh in 1645. The Johnston tartan was registered in the mid-nineteenth century, and probably derives from the Aberdeenshire branch of the family.

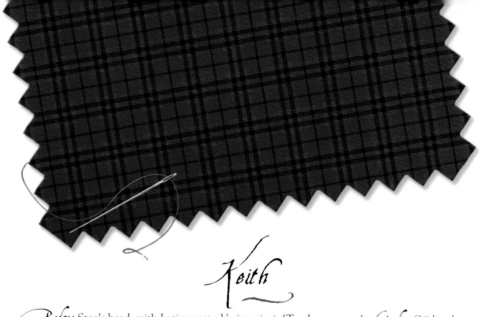

# Keith

**Badge:** Stag's head, with Latin motto *Veritas vincit* (Truth conquers)   **Gaelic:** *Céitheach*

The Keith story begins when a Norman knight, Hervey (d. *c.* 1196), was granted the lands of Keith in Banffshire by King David I (r. 1124–53) in 1150. By the fourteenth century, the Keith clan chief had taken the title of 'Great Marischal of Scotland', an honorary title that brought responsibility for the Royal Regalia of Scotland and for the king's protection while he was attending parliament. Sir William Keith (d. *c.* 1475) was appointed as Earl Marischal in 1458, a title the Keith family held until the early eighteenth century.

# Kennedy

*Badge:* Dolphin, with French motto *Avise la fin* (Consider the end)
*Gaelic:* Ceanadach (Ugly head)

The Kennedy clan began with one Cunedda, who settled in south-western Scotland during the fifth century AD. During the later Middle Ages, the Kennedys rose as a powerful Lowland clan in Ayrshire. They sided with Robert the Bruce (r. 1306–29) against the Comyns and during the Wars of Independence, and Gilbert Kennedy (c. 1406–c. 1479) was ennobled as the 1st Lord Kennedy in 1457. Sir David Kennedy (1478–1513) was appointed Earl of Cassilis in 1509. One of their greatest physical legacies is Culzean Castle, designed by the famous Scottish architect Robert Adam (1728–92).

# Kerr

**Badge:** Shining sun, with Latin motto *Sero sed serio* (Late but in earnest)
**Gaelic:** MacGilleChiar

This Border family established itself from the twelfth century, but it was not destined to be a harmonious clan. The Kerrs established themselves in Roxburghshire, Ayrshire and Aberdeenshire, but the descendants of two brothers – Ralph and John – split into mutually hostile branches at Ferniehurst and Cessford respectively. Kerrs were prominent players in Scotland's border conflicts, the Kerrs of Cessford becoming wardens of the marches, while both lines attained various noble ranks. The name itself is related to the *ciar*, Gaelic for 'dark complexioned'.

## Kilgour

*Gaelic: Cille Ghobhar*

Taking their name from the parish of Kilgour in Fife, the Kilgours are a sept of the MacDuff clan, and they spread widely throughout the United Kingdom, not just Scotland. Earliest records, dating from the sixteenth century, show an ecclesiastical calling – Sir Thomas Kilgore was recorded as a palace chaplain at Falkland Palace in 1528, and a later ancestor, John, served in Aberdeen Cathedral. During the nineteenth century, an exodus of Kilgours meant that the name became very common in Australia and the United States. Three tartans are currently registered, although the origins of the patterns are uncertain.

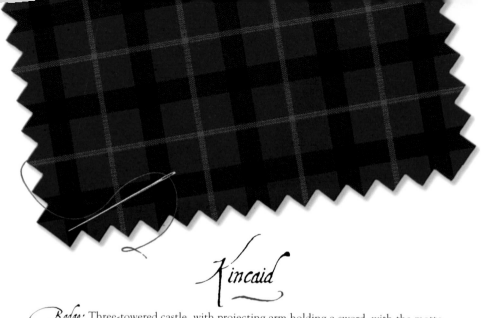

# Kincaid

**Badge:** Three-towered castle, with projecting arm holding a sword, with the motto
'This I'll defend' **Gaelic:** Ceann Cadha

The Kincaid badge's martial connotations are perfectly justified. In 1296, the clan lord led his warriors in a successful action to retake Edinburgh Castle. For this, the Laird of Kincaid was appointed Constable of the Castle. The Kincaids' ancestral lands are in Stirlingshire and, from the thirteenth century, they grew in power and territorial extent. From the seventeenth century, their political futures became more complicated, supporting the royalists in the Civil War and the Jacobites post-1680, the latter alliance leading to many Kincaids emigrating to America in the eighteenth century.

# Kinnaird

**Motto:** 'Wandering lights deceive'  **Gaelic:** Ceann Àrd

The barony of Kinnaird was established in the 1100s in Perthshire, and instances of the family name are found from that time in many variations, including Kinnard, Kynharde, Kynnard, Kennard, Kinnart, Kynnart, Kinzerd and Kynarde. According to historians, the clan is descended from Rudulphus Ruffus, a Norman nobleman who received territories in the Carse of Gowrie from William I the Lion (*c.* 1142–1214), the elevated nature of the land yielding the Gaelic word *Ceann Àrd* (high promontory). Following the religious conflicts of the eighteenth century, many Kinnairds emigrated to America and Ireland.

# Kinnison

*Gaelic:* MacConain or MacCoinnich

The Gaelic of Kinnison translates as 'Son of Conan', the name likely referring to Conan of Glenerochy, in turn the son of Henry, Earl of Atholl. Regarded as a sept of the MacFarlanes, the Kinnisons settled in Perthshire, where the name appears in variations that include Kinnieson, Cunieson and MacConich. Two tartans on the Scottish Register of Tartans are listed to the Kennison and Kinnieson names. Both are modern tartans, the former registered in 2002 and the latter in the 1960s. The Kinnieson tartan is likely to be a personal rather than a clan tartan.

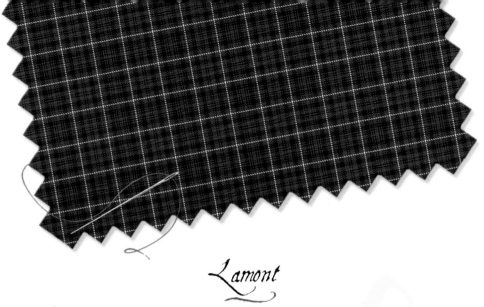

## Lamont

*Badge:* Open right hand, palm facing forward, with Latin motto *Ne parcas nec spernas* (Neither spare nor dispose) *Gaelic:* MacLaomainn

The Lamonts of Argyll settled in their ancestral lands during the early thirteenth century, and the clan grew upon the foundation of one Lamont, who lived in Cowal in the 1230s. The Lamont name appears in several thirteenth-century charters, and the early chiefs of the clan were referred to as 'The Great MacLamont of all Cowal', where they exercised judicial authority over their local area. The lowest point in Lamont history came in 1646, when Campbell forces massacred more than 200 Lamonts in a churchyard at Dunoon, part of the Wars of the Three Kingdoms.

## Largs

*Badge:* Three thistles and a Viking ship with the Norwegian lion on the sail

*Gaelic:* An Leargaidh Ghallda

The district tartan of Largs, a coastal town in Ayrshire, was designed during the early 1950s by Sidney Samuels and was officially registered in 1983. Largs has also acquired a dress tartan – a 1972 issue from Highland Queen Sportswear of Toronto – and another district tartan emerged in the early 1980s. The town of Largs's most famous event is the Battle of Largs in October 1263. During this battle, the Scottish forces of Alexander III (r. 1249–86) crushed the Viking armada of Haakon IV of Norway (r. 1217–63).

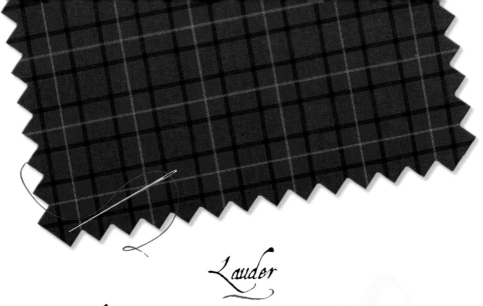

## Lauder

*Badge:* Sentinel above a tower, with Latin motto *Turris prudentia custos*
(Prudence is the guardian of the tower)

The Lauder name relates to the town in Berwickshire, and the earliest known ancestor is one Sir Robert de Laudre, a Norman nobleman who settled in Scotland in the second half of the eleventh century. The Lauder lands were granted by Malcolm III 'Canmore' (r. 1059–93), following the solid performance of Robert at the Battle of Birnham Wood in 1056. Notable Lauders include Robert, who fought at the Battle of Stirling Bridge in 1297, and William (c. 1380–1425), who was the Bishop of Glasgow and Lord Chancellor of Scotland during the fifteenth century.

## Leask

Arguments over the origins of the surname Leask are still ongoing, with theories ranging from the Anglo-Saxon word *lisse* ('happy') to the name of a Gaelic chief called *Liscus*. What we do know, however, is that, during the fourteenth century, a William Leaske was granted the lands of Leskgoroune by King David II (1329–71), William becoming the clan's first chief. History has not always been kind to the Leasks. They suffered heavy losses in the sixteenth-century wars against the English, including the death of the 5th chief at Flodden in 1513 and, during the seventeenth century, financial ruin meant that the 13th chief had to relinquish his estates. The tartan dates from the 1980s.

# Lennox

**Badge:** Crossed broadswords behind a swan's neck and head, with the motto 'I'll defend'

**Gaelic:** An Leamhnachd (Smooth stream)

This tartan dates back to the sixteenth century, authenticated from a contemporary portrait. The Celtic ancestors of the Lennox clan held the earldom of Lennox from the twelfth century, the first recorded earl being Ailín, who lived in the middle of the twelfth century. The 5th earl, Malcolm (d. 1333), was a strong ally of Robert the Bruce (r. 1306–29). The Lennox clan was deeply connected with the Stewart monarchy, with Lord John Stewart of Darnley (d. 1495) becoming the Earl of Lennox in 1488. Charles II (r. 1660–85) himself later took the Earl of Lennox title.

## Leslie

*Badge:* Demi-griffin, with the motto 'Grip fast'   *Gaelic:* Mac an Fhleisdeir

Originating in the lands of Leslie in Aberdeenshire, this clan enters the history books in the eleventh century in the form of Flemish noble Bartolf. Bartolf rose to become the governor of Edinburgh Castle and took control of territories in Fife, Angus and Aberdeenshire. Several lines of Leslies developed in Scotland, and they were known for producing great military commanders such as Alexander Leslie (1582–1661), who served the Swedish king/commander Gustavus Adolphus of Sweden (r. 1611–32) during the Thirty Years' War, and the Covenanter General David Leslie (1601–82).

# Lindsay

*Badge:* Swan rising from a coronet, with French motto *Endure fort* (Endure bravely)

The Lindsays appear to be another clan of Norman descent, who settled into Scotland during the eleventh century (the name derives from Limesay in Normandy), although some histories suggest an earlier Nordic descent. The earliest reference to a Lindsay is to Baldric de Lindsay, while Sir Walter de Lindsay is recorded as the Baron of Luffness in the 1160s, being granted extensive lands by David I (r. 1124–53). The Lindsays steadily divided into two major branches – the Crawfords and the Balcarres – with both branches having their own earls.

## Livingstone

*Badge:* Demi-savage holding a serpent and club, with French motto *Si je puis* (If I can)

*Gaelic:* Mac an Léigh

Undoubtedly the most famous of the Livingstones was Dr David Livingstone (1813–73), the doctor and missionary who became an international name on account of his African explorations. Other great members of the Livingstone clan include Sir James Livingstone, appointed the Great Chamberlain of Scotland in 1458, and Alexander Livingstone (d. 1623), who became the Earl of Linlithgow in 1600 (although the family subsequently lost land and title after the Jacobite uprising in 1715). The Livingstone clan tartan dates from the early twentieth century, and there are three modern tartans for the Livingstones of Australia.

## Loch Ness

*Gaelic:* Loch Nis

Loch Ness is famous the world over for its 'monster', a large aquatic creature believed by some to be a plesiosaur, a remnant of the dinosaur age, while many others dismiss the apparent sightings as hoaxes or optical illusions. Whatever the truth of the Loch Ness monster, it is apparent that 'sightings' have occurred for centuries. The earliest mention is believed to have come from St Columba who apparently confronted the creature back in the sixth century. Regardless of the monster, Loch Ness is a powerful and evocative place, and it has two district tartans to its name. The two are contrasting, with one being a warm fusion of green, red, black and white, while the other is dominated by watery blue tones.

## Lockhart

*Badge:* Boar's head, with Latin motto *Corda serrata fero* (I open locked hearts)

Historians provide several different explanations for the origins of the Lockharts, ascribing either English, Norman or Danish blood to the clan beginnings. What is certain is that, by the twelfth century, Locards had settled in Lanarkshire. Sir Symon Locard (1300–71) was famously the key-holder for the casket that contained Robert the Bruce's heart, which Symon unsuccessfully attempted to transport to the Holy Land in accordance with Bruce's wishes. In honour of the attempt, Symon changed his surname to Lockhart, a name that has remained in the clan to this day.

## Logan

**Badge:** Heart pierced with a nail, with Latin motto *Hoc majorum virtus*
(This is the valour of my ancestors) **Gaelic:** Lòganach

The Logans are an armigerous clan (*see* page 108), originally from the lands of Logan in Ayrshire. Several instances of the Logan name are recorded during the thirteenth century, appearing on land records as early as 1204, plus three instances on the Ragman Rolls in 1296 (including the variant spelling Logyn). The Logans subsequently divided into Highland and Lowland branches, with the former associated with the MacLennan clan. Some of the vivid figures from Logan history include Sir Robert and Sir Logan, knights killed alongside Black Douglas (*c.* 1286–1330) in 1330.

## Lorne

*Gaelic:* Latharna

Situated on the west coast of Scotland between Argyll and Lochaber, the district of Lorne has acquired eight tartans, dating from the late nineteenth century to the present day. Many of them are associated with the Marquis of Lorne, the primary Lorne tartan of 1871 being related to the Campbell sett. In 1871, John Douglas Campbell (1845–1914), the Marquis of Lorne, married Queen Victoria's daughter Louise. The actual Lorne name is held to derive from a group of Scots who settled in Argyll during the late sixth century. The group was supposedly led by Fergus Mór mac Eirc whose brother, Loarn, was the source of the district name.

*iby*

## Lumsden

*Badge:* Arm and hand holding a sword, with Latin motto *Amor patitur moras*
(Love endures delays)

The Lumsden name has its origins in the manor of Lumsden in the Berwickshire village of Coldingham. King Edgar (r. 1074–1107) granted the manor to the priory he founded in 1098, although the personal name Lumsden does not appear until later, in the thirteenth century. The original founders of the Lumsdens were brothers Roger and Adam, whose names appear on the Ragman Rolls in 1296. In c. 1328, Gilbert de Lumsden gained, through marriage, lands at Blaerne, which, with its imposing castle, became the main clan seat.

## Mac Alister

**Badge:** Right hand holding a dagger, with Latin motto *Fortiter* (Boldly)

**Gaelic:** MacAlasdair

The MacAlisters have their ancestral home in Kintyre, and their progenitor is Alasdair Mór, son of Donald of Islay. As such, the MacAlisters are classed as a branch of the Donald clan. Dominant elements of the clan were the MacAlisters of Loup, who came to be a powerful presence in Kintyre, and the MacAlisters of Tarbert, who acted as Constables of Tarbert Castle on Loch Fyne, on the west coast of Argyll and Bute. There are also the MacAlistairs of Glenbarr, Argyll, who acquired major landholdings during the eighteenth and nineteenth centuries.

# Mac Alpine

**Badge:** Saracen's head, bloodied, with Gaelic motto *Cuinich bas Alpan*
(Remember the death of Alpin) **Gaelic:** MacAilpein

The antiquity of the MacAlpines has few rivals in clan history. The founder of the clan was King Alpin, a ruler of Dalriada during the ninth century. His son, Kenneth (810–58), brought about the union of the kingdoms of Picts and Scots, a vital step in the creation of Scotland. Today, the MacAlpines are a 'landless' clan, although, traditionally, their territory was around Dunstaffnage near Oban in Argyll. Historically, they were septs of other clans, but the MacAlpine name has still produced some great figures, including the construction giant Sir Robert McAlpine (1847–1934).

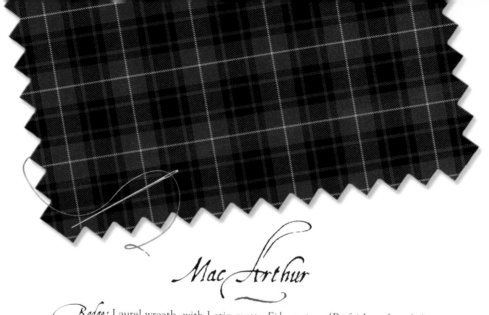

## Mac Arthur

*Badge:* Laurel wreath, with Latin motto *Fide et opera* (By faith and works)

*Gaelic:* MacArtair

The greatest MacArthur of modern times is the US commander General Douglas MacArthur, an epic and controversial figure during the Pacific War in 1941–45 and the Korean War in 1950–53. Power perhaps runs in the veins of this clan, as some claim descent from King Arthur himself. More tangibly, the MacArthurs established themselves with the chief Artair mac Artair, who was granted estates in Argyll by Robert the Bruce. A critical event in MacArthur history was the execution of chief Iain (d. 1427) by James I (r. 1406–37), which resulted in the clan scattering over wider territories.

## MacAuley

**Badge:** Antique boot, with Latin motto *Dulce periculum* (Peril is sweet)
**Gaelic:** MacAmhlaigh

The MacAuley name actually embraces several different families and clans, some quite unconnected with one another. For example, the MacAulays of Lewis are distinct from the MacAulays of Ardencaple (also spelt Ardincaple), who have their lands in Argyll and Skye. The former MacAulays take their name from the Gaelic *MacAmhlaigh*, meaning 'son of Olaf', while the latter relate their name to the family seat in Ardencaple. MacAuleys also have strong historical associations with the MacGregors, hence one of their tartans is listed as 'MacAuley (MacGregor)'.

## MacBean

**Badge:** Demi-cat rampant, with the motto 'Touch not the cat bot [without] a glove'

**Gaelic:** MacBheathain (Son of the lively one)

The MacBean/MacBain name appears in the mid-fourteenth century with references to Beathan mac Mhaolmhoire and Maolmhoire mac Bheathain. We know that the clan formed part of the Chattan Confederation, and supported Robert the Bruce during the Wars of Independence. Originally from Lochaber, the family then spread widely, but lost a lot of land during the seventeenth and eighteenth centuries, both through land sales and the effects of the Jacobite rebellions, the latter resulting in many MacBeans/MacBains being deported overseas to the American colonies.

# MacBeth

**Badge:** Mailed arm holding a sword  **Gaelic:** Mac Bheatha (Son of life)

The historical MacBeth, King of the Scots from 1040–57, has only a loose connection to the harried and disturbed character of Shakespeare's eponymous play. He was the son of Findláech mac Ruaidrí (d. 1020), Mormaer of Moray, and Doada, the daughter of Malcolm II (r. 1005–34), and was married to the granddaughter of Kenneth III (r. 997–1005). He ascended to the throne of the Scots after killing his predecessor Duncan (r. 1034–40) at Pitgaveny in 1040. The name was reasonably common, but its variants, which include Bethune (*see* page 33) and MacVeigh, obscure the ancestral lines of the family.

## MacBride

*Gaelic:* MacGilleBrìde (Son of the servant of St Bride or Bridget)

The MacBrides take their name from St Bride/Brigid/Bridget (c. 451–525), an Irish patron saint who had considerable influence in Scotland as well as her home country. Seen as a sept of the MacDonalds, the MacBrides came to have a particularly widespread distribution across Scotland, being found as far afield as the Hebrides and Ayrshire. The tartan associated with the MacBrides was created in 1992 by Harry Lindley, specifically for a Captain Stuart C. MacBride (the colours reflect his personal arms).

## MacCallum

*Badge:* Castle, with Latin motto *In ardua tendit* (He has attempted difficult things)
*Gaelic:* MacCaluim

The MacCallum tartan was designed during the nineteenth century. An initial sett was prepared based on the memories of old people from Argyllshire, but a more accurate sett was designed against earlier antique samples. The MacCallum clan was centred in Lorn in Argyllshire by the advent of the fourteenth century, its name meaning a follower of St Columba (*c.* 521–97). From Argyll, the MacCallums then acquired lands in Craignish and Lochavich. Note that, during the late eighteenth century, Alexander MacCallum (d. 1787), 9th Lord of Poltalloch, changed his name to Malcolm.

## MacColl

*Badge:* Six-pointed star with the horns of a crescent, with Latin motto *Justi ut sidera fulgent* (They shine like stars) *Gaelic:* MacColla

A branch of the Donald clan, the MacColls hail from the Loch Fyne region of Scotland. MacColl history is soaked in blood, particularly in the bitter feud with the MacGregors, which in turn brought them into conflict with the MacPhersons. This enmity led to a massacre in 1602, when a raiding party of MacColls was trapped at Drum Nachder and killed. MacColls also suffered further heavy losses during the Jacobite rebellions. A famous member of the clan was Evan MacColl (1808–98), a renowned Gaelic poet.

# MacCorquodale

*Motto:* Vivat rex (Let the King live)    *Gaelic:* MacCorcadail

The MacCorquodales are often held to be a sept of the MacLeods of Lewis, although many historians now question this idea, pointing to the fact that the MacCorquodales are likely to predate the MacLeods and that the MacCorquodale name does not appear in MacLeod histories. The ancestral homelands of the MacCorquodales are around Loch Tromlee, and the name itself derives from the Old Norse *Thorketill* ('Thor's kettle'), in Gaelic rendered as *MacCorcadail*. The chiefs were known as the Barons MacCorquodale of Phantelane ('White Island'). The last chief died during the eighteenth century.

## MacDiarmid

*Gaelic:* MacDhiarmaid

The MacDiarmids are a sept of the Campbells and, during their early history, seem mostly confined to Argyll, particularly Lorn, Lochaber and Glenlyon. The origins of the name lie in the Old Irish *diarmit* (freeman), and is seen in several variations, including MacDermot. In terms of clan tartans, there are currently four tartans registered, all classified as clan/family setts. The basic MacDiarmid tartan design was recorded in *The Tartans of the Clans and Septs of Scotland* (1906) by H. Whyte. A tartan known as MacDiarmid Dress dates back to the 1830s.

## MacDonald

**Badge:** Mailed fist holding a cross-crosslet, with Latin motto
*Per mare per terras* (By sea and land)  **Gaelic:** *MacDhòmhnaill*

No clan has exceeded the MacDonalds in power. The clan's progenitor was Somerled, King of the Isles (d. 1164). Somerled had three sons, who formed the beginning of various MacDonald lines, the clan in total taking its name from one of the sons, Donald. Rather than being one homogenous MacDonald clan, numerous powerful branches had developed by the end of the Middle Ages (see separate entries for discussion of these branches). They covered a large territorial area, from the Highlands to the Lowlands, and became one of the most powerful forces in Scottish politics outside royalty.

## MacDonald, Flora

*Badge:* Triple-towered castle with an armoured arm holding a sword, with the motto
'My hope is constant in thee'  *Gaelic: Fionnghal NicDhòmhnaill*

Flora MacDonald (1722–90) is one of many legendary clan figures. Born in South Uist in 1722, in 1746, Flora helped Bonnie Prince Charlie (1720–88), a fugitive after the Battle of Culloden, to escape by sea, the pair travelling to the coast with Charles dressed as an Irish maid. For this, Flora was arrested and imprisoned in the Tower of London, but released under a general amnesty in 1747. She later emigrated to America with her husband Allan MacDonald of Kingsburgh, fleeing from North Carolina to Nova Scotia to escape anti-British rebels, but returned to Scotland in 1779.

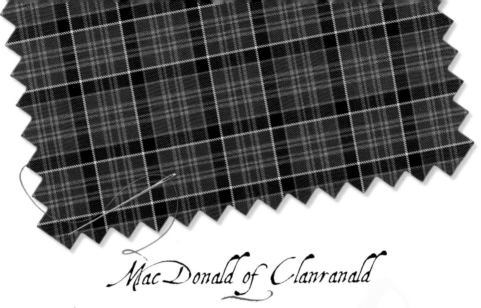

## MacDonald of Clanranald

*Badge:* Triple-towered castle with an armoured arm holding a sword, with the motto
'My hope is constant in thee' *Gaelic:* Mac Mhic Ailein

The MacDonalds of Clanranald line began in the twelfth century with Raghnall (d. 1207), son of King Somerled (d. 1164), and they consolidated their landholdings in Moidart, Glengarry, Lochaber and Glencoe. This branch of the MacDonalds was frequently locked in feuds with other branches, and disputes over the chieftainship in the sixteenth century led to physical battles for control. In 1544, John of Moidart and Ranald Gallda fought each other to win the chieftainship, John winning the battle and killing Ranald. Later Clanranalds fought for the Stuarts and the Jacobites.

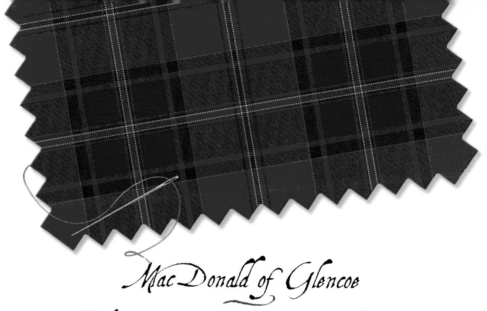

## MacDonald of Glencoe

*Badge:* Phoenix, with the motto 'In hope I byde'  *Gaelic:* Mac Iain

Described by the government of William III (r. 1650–1702) as 'the worst [clan] in all the Highlands', the MacDonalds of Glencoe gained a renegade reputation following events in 1692. Chief Alexander MacDonald of Glencoe (d. 1692) failed to sign an oath of allegiance to William of Orange (r. 1689–1702) on 1 January, purely through accident and not intention, but his clan was targeted for retribution. On 15 February 1692, a force of Campbells massacred 38 MacDonalds at Glencoe. The enmity generated by this event lasted for generations.

## MacDonald of Sleat

*Badge:* Armoured fist holding a cross-crosslet, with Latin motto
*Per mare per terras* (By sea and land) *Gaelic:* Mac Ùisdein

The MacDonalds of Sleat, a peninsula on the Isle of Skye, were established by Hugh MacDonald (d. 1498), son of Alexander, Earl of Ross and 3rd Lord of the Isles. After 1494, Hugh held his lands under royal charter, the position of Lord of the Isles being abolished, although subsequent generations of the MacDonalds did attempt to reclaim the lordship, resulting in frequent conflict between clans, chiefs and crown. Today, Lord MacDonald of Sleat is regarded as the chief of Clan MacDonald. The vivid red MacDonald of Sleat tartan was designed in the eighteenth century.

# MacDonald of Staffa

*Badge:* Armoured fist holding a cross-crosslet, with Latin motto
*Per mare per terras* (By sea and land) *Gaelic:* MacDhòmhnaill Stafa

The MacDonalds of Staffa take their name from the island of Staffa, which in turn was named after the Old Norse for 'stave island'. It is a remote island off the west coast of Scotland near Mull (and the location of the impressive Fingal's Cave), owned in the early nineteenth century by MacDonald of Staffa, although the island itself was deserted by this time. Little is known about the lives of the inhabitants of Staffa, despite the tourism that developed during the nineteenth and twentieth centuries.

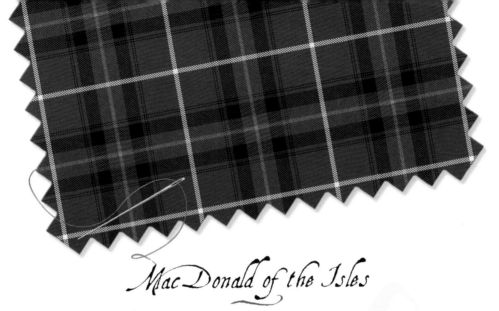

## MacDonald of the Isles

*Badge:* Armoured fist holding a cross-crosslet, with Latin motto
*Per mare per terras* (By sea and land)  *Gaelic:* MacDhòmhnaill nan Eilean

After the position of Lord of the Isles (*see* page 181) was abolished in the late fifteenth century, there was a prolonged state of war, as various individuals vied to re-establish themselves as chief. This situation rumbled on until 1610, until the clans made an agreement to keep the peace in the islands. The MacDonald of the Isles tartan is first recorded in the *Vestiarium Scoticum* of 1842, and it is today classified as a fashion tartan, not being connected with a specific clan.

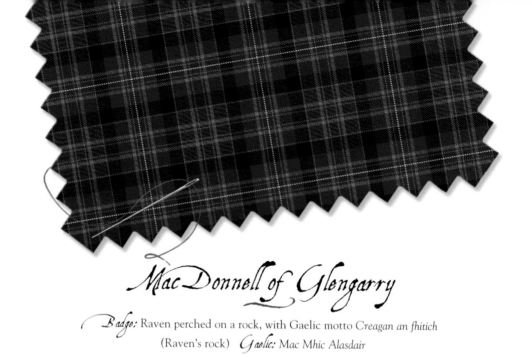

# MacDonnell of Glengarry

**Badge:** Raven perched on a rock, with Gaelic motto *Creagan an fhitich* (Raven's rock) **Gaelic:** Mac Mhic Alasdair

The MacDonnells of Glengarry share an ancestor with the MacDonalds in the form of Ranald of the Isles (1300–86). One of his sons, Donald (d. 1420), became chief of the MacDonells of Glengarry, and his other son, Alan (d.1430), King of the Isles. The chieftainship of the MacDonnells of Glengarry extends to this day, and the clan has five registered tartans bearing its name. Three of these, including the one shown here, are based on patterns discovered in the early nineteenth century, one is from the early twentieth century, and a modern dress tartan was registered in 2002.

# MacDonnell of Keppoch

**Badge:** Three-towered castle surmounted by an armoured arm, holding a sword, with the motto 'My hope is constant in thee' **Gaelic:** Mac Mhic Raghnaill

The MacDonnells of Keppoch are another part of the complex tapestry of clans and septs that form the MacDonalds, with their progenitor being Alasdair Carrach, who reigned as first chief of the Keppochs from *c.* 1390–*c.* 1443. The MacDonnells of Keppoch came to blows with other local clans, the rivals extending claims over the same territories. At the Battle of the Shirts in 1544, Clanranald MacDonalds (of which the MacDonnells were a branch) and Camerons fought warriors from clans Fraser and Grant. The outcome of the battle is uncertain.

## MacDougall

**Badge:** Arm in armour, holding a cross-crosslet, with Latin motto
*Vincere et mori* (To win or die)  **Gaelic:** *MacDhùghaill*

Another son of Somerled (d. 1164), King of the Isles, was Dugald, the progenitor of this major Highland clan. His territories were extensive and included large parts of Argyll plus the islands of Mull, Tiree, Jura, Coll and Lismore. During the fourteenth century, the MacDougalls were in bitter opposition to Robert the Bruce (r. 1306–29) on account of their marital connections with the Comyns (Bruce murdered John 'the Red' Comyn in 1306). Through battle and problems finding heirs, the MacDougalls lost many of their ancestral lands, which were not restored until the eighteenth century.

# MacDuff

**Badge:** Demi-lion rampant holding a dagger, with Latin motto *Deus juvat* (God helps)
**Gaelic:** MacDhubhaich

The MacDuffs originated with the Celtic Earls of Fife – the first earl aided in the ascent of Malcolm Canmore (r. 1059–93) to the throne in 1059, helping in the overthrow of MacBeth. The clan's influence grew from this event onwards, and the chiefs of the MacDuff clan had the legal right to enthrone Scottish kings on the Stone of Destiny (a block of sandstone used in the coronation of Scottish, English and British monarchs). There are at least two dozen MacDuff tartans in existence today, most dating from the nineteenth and early twentieth centuries.

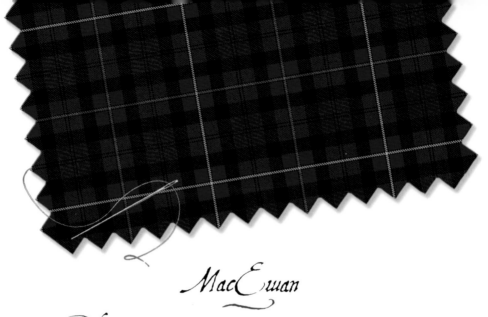

## MacEwan

**Badge:** The trunk of an oak tree showing new growth, with Latin motto
*Reviresco* (I grow strong again)  **Gaelic:** MacEoghainn

The MacEwans are a venerable Scottish clan. In the fifteenth century, they held lands around Otter on Loch Fyne, Argyll, and later formed the Siol Gillevray alliance along with the MacLachlans (*see* page 209) and the MacNeills. (It was the thirteenth-century Ewen of Otter, however, who stands as founder of the clan.) The MacEwans also struck up close relations with the Campbells, so much so that, in 1432, Swene MacEwan, the ninth MacEwan chief, gave the ancestral lands to them, an act confirmed by James V (*r.* 1513–42) in 1513.

# MacFadyen

*Gaelic:* MacPhaidein (Son of Little Patrick)

The MacFadyens seem to have settled in Scotland from Ireland during the fourteenth century. They became particularly associated with the craft of goldsmithing, taking their skills on an itinerant basis throughout Scotland, but putting down established businesses at Mull. They were a sept of the MacLaines of Lochbuie, a place granted to them by a charter from John, 1st Lord of the Isles. The name has several variations to this day, including MacFadzean and MacPhedrean, and there are multiple tartans associated with the names, most of nineteenth- and twentieth-century derivation.

## MacFarlane

**Badge:** Demi-savage holding a sheath of arrows and a crown, with the motto 'This I'll defend'
**Gaelic:** MacPhàrlain

Loch Lomond has been the ancestral home of many clans, including the MacGregors, Buchanans, Colquhouns, Cunninghams and Stewarts, with the MacFarlanes occupying the west bank. The name derives from Bartholomew (*Pàrlan* in Gaelic), the great grandson of Gilchrist, a thirteenth-century Earl of Lennox. The MacFarlanes were a warlike and frequently troublesome clan, fighting against Mary, Queen of Scots (1542–57), and wielding their swords in battles such as Flodden (1513), Pinkie (1547) and Langside (1568). The clan was outlawed and dispossessed in the seventeenth century, many of the clan emigrating to America.

# Mac Fie

**Badge:** Demi-lion rampant, with Latin motto *Pro rege* (For the king)
**Gaelic:** MacDhubhShìth or Mac a' Phì

The MacFie clan (also spelt as MacPhee or MacDuffie) hails from the Isle of Colonsay in Argyll. A MacFie signature appears on a charter of 1463, and Chief MacFie of Colonsay was one of nine who signed the Statutes of Iona in 1609, by which the crown sought to control clan activities. Later in the seventeenth century, the MacFies lost Colonsay to the Campbells, many of them then moving to Lochaber. A famous MacFie was Ewen MacPhee, a nineteenth-century Scottish outlaw who lived on an island in Loch Quoich until imprisoned for sheep-stealing.

# MacGill

*Gaelic:* Mac a' Ghoill

The MacGill clan originates from western Scotland, originally settling in the thirteenth century in Galloway in the southern Lowlands before migrating north to the Island of Jura in the Inner Hebrides in the eighteenth century. The Gaelic form of the name, *Mac a' Ghoill*, meaning 'Son of a stranger', reflects their migrant status. One particularly famous MacGill was James MacGill (1744–1813). Born in Glasgow, the son of an ironsmith, he emigrated to Canada in 1766 and rose to become an industrialist and civic figure, founding the educational establishment that is today MacGill University, Montreal.

# MacGillivray

**Badge:** Cat, with the motto 'Touch not the cat bot [without] a glove'  **Gaelic:** MacGilleBhrath

As the clan motto suggests, the MacGillivrays were once part of the Clan Chattan (*see* page 67). Their origins go back to the thirteenth century. The current arms of the MacGillivrays were matriculated in 1967, although they date back to the seventeenth century and their Chattan associations. Before this time, however, the armorial bearings consisted of a stag's head, either in profile or facing straight on. MacGillivray lands were originally Morven, Mull and Lochaber, later moving into Strathnairn.

## MacGregor

**Badge:** Crowned lion's head, with Gaelic motto *'S rioghail mo dhream* (Royal is my race)
**Gaelic:** MacGriogair

The MacGregors are one of the more famous, and infamous, of the Scottish clans, producing such mythologized warrior outlaws as Rob Roy MacGregor (1671–1743). Legend has it that they descended from Griogar, a ninth-century King of the Scots. Their territory was originally the borderlands of Argyll and Perthshire, but events made it hard for them to hang on to their lands. They were frequently at war with the Campbells, and the clan was eventually outlawed in 1603, restored under Charles II (r. 1660–85), then outlawed again by William of Orange (r. 1689–1702), a ban that lasted until 1775.

## MacGregor of Glenstrae

**Badge:** Crowned lion's head, with Gaelic motto *'S rìoghail mo dhream* (Royal is my race)
**Gaelic:** MacGriogair Ghlinn Sreith

The MacGregors produced several branches of the clan, the three principal ones being those of Glengyle, Glenlochy and Glenstrae. The tartan of the last branch is represented here. There are two tartans associated with the MacGregors of Glenstrae. One is described in the *Vestiarium Scoticum* during the nineteenth century (although there is no illustration provided), and the other was shown by James Logan in his collection of material entitled *The Scottish Gael*, written around 1826 and published in 1831. There is also a Rob Roy MacGregor tartan, whose design dates back to 1704.

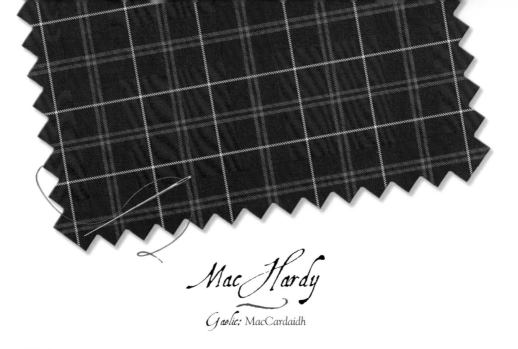

## Mac Hardy

*Gaelic:* MacCardaidh

The MacHardy, or MacHardie, clan came from lands in Cogarth, Strathdon, in Aberdeenshire. Although the first recorded appearance of the name dates from 1560, its ancestry is certainly much older. The name itself comes from the Gaelic *Mac a' Chardaidh*, apparently meaning 'Son of the sloe', or from *hardi* ('bold'). Compensating for their small size, the MacHardys made alliances with the Clan Chattan, the Farquharsons, Mackintoshes and others. During the eighteenth and nineteenth centuries, many emigrated abroad or to England, dropping the 'Mac' part of the name to form 'Hardy'.

## MacIan

**Badge:** Phoenix, with the motto 'In hope I byde' **Gaelic:** MacIain

The MacIans were never a single unified clan, but rather a collection of Scottish families sharing a common name (or variants of the name, including MacIain, MacKeane and MacKain). The different families trace their ancestry back to contrasting origins. The MacIans of Ardnamurchan, for example, see their progenitor as Eion Sprangach, son of the thirteenth-century Lord of the Isles, Angus Mòr (d. *c.* 1296). Other MacIans, specifically those of Glencoe, were branches of the MacDonald clan. The current MacIan tartan is another product of the nineteenth century, dating from 1842.

## MacInnes

*Badge:* Bee feeding from a thistle, with Latin motto *E labore dulcedoa*
(Pleasure comes from work) *Gaelic:* MacAonghais

With origins reflected in the Gaelic name of this family, MacInnes historians believe that the clan is descended from Oenghus, one of the founders of Dalriada in the fifth century and chief of one of Dalriada's original tribes. Although there are question marks over this narrative, the MacInneses are certainly an extremely old family, settling in Argyll in the early medieval period, around Morven and Ardnamurchan. The MacInnes clan also served as constables of Kinlochaline Castle, which was burned down during the Civil Wars in 1644 by the MacDonalds.

# MacInroy

*Gaelic:* Mac Iain Ruaidh

The MacInroy family tartan dates back to the eighteenth century, with the sett discovered in a pattern book of the famous Scottish weavers, Wilsons of Bannockburn, who were founded around 1770 near Stirling. At the time of writing, there are three main MacInroy tartans – MacInroy, MacInroy of Lude and MacInroy Hunting, the MacInroy of Lude tartan reserved exclusively for the Lude branch of the clan. MacInroy ancestors established themselves in Straloch and Pitlochry in the sixteenth century, and were allied with the Dukes of Atholl, the Fergusons and the Stewarts.

## Macintosh

*Badge:* Cat, with the motto 'Touch not the cat bot (without) a glove'   *Gaelic:* Mac an Tòisich

The prevalence of the Macintosh/Mackintosh name is suggested by the 23 tartans currently registered in the Scottish Register of Tartans. They were part of the Clan Chattan confederation from the late thirteenth century; the clan was originally established around the lands of Petty a century earlier, their founders being from the royal house of Duff. Recent famous descendants include Charles Macintosh (1766–1843), who invented a fabric waterproofing technique that produced the Macintosh raincoat, and also the Glasgow-born architect and painter Charles Rennie Mackintosh (1868–1928).

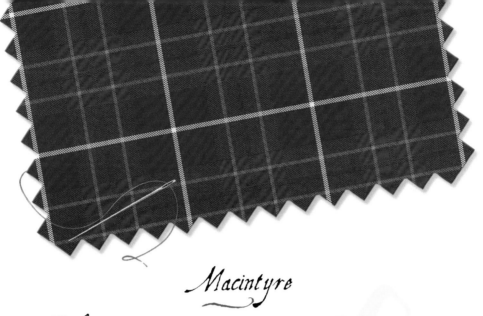

## Macintyre

*Badge:* Hand holding a dagger, with Latin motto *Per ardua* (Through struggles)
*Gaelic:* Mac an t-Saoir

The Gaelic *Mac an t-Saoir* ('Son of the carpenter') refers to one Macarill, who was the nephew of the twelfth-century Lord of the Isles, Somerled (d. 1164). The story goes that Macarill drilled holes in a ship belonging to King Olav of Norway (*c.* 1080–1153). When the ship started to sink, Macarill said he would fix the problem if the king promised his daughter's hand in marriage to Somerled. The story appears fanciful, but the early Macintyres were known as carpenters, moving from the Hebrides to mainland Scotland in the thirteenth century.

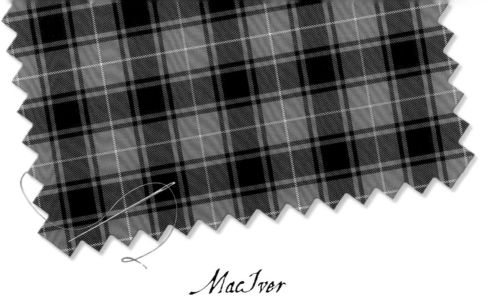

## MacIver

**Badge:** Boar's head, with Latin motto *Nunquam obliviscar* (I shall never forget)
**Gaelic:** MacIomhair

The MacIvers enter Scottish history as warriors, fighting for Alexander II (r. 1214–49), for which they were granted the lands of Glassary. Later MacIver history was violent – at the Battle of Bealach na Bròige in 1452, many MacIvers were killed in battle with rival clans. The clan progressively broke up into several different regional families. The branches in Argyll largely renamed themselves Campbell after political arrangements made between Iver MacIver of Lergachonzie and Archibald Campbell, 5th Earl of Argyll (c. 1532–73), although other branches kept the MacIver name.

## Mackay

*Badge:* Hand holding a dagger, with Latin motto *Manu forti* (With a strong hand)

*Gaelic:* MacAoidh

The Mackays were established in the north-west of Scotland, around Strathnever, by the fourteenth century. Through their support of Robert the Bruce (r. 1306–29), the clan gained considerable power and influence. They frequently fought against other clans such as the Sinclairs, Keiths, Rosses and Sutherlands, their martial might backed by an army that numbered more than four thousand by the fifteenth century. They later fought against the Jacobites, and Mackays are seen in every major British conflict from the Thirty Years' War (1618–48) to the Falklands War in 1982.

# Mackellar

*Badge:* Boar's head, with Latin motto *Ne obliviscaris* (Do not forget)

*Gaelic:* MacEalair (Son of Hilary)

The Mackellar ancestral lands are in Argyllshire. The clan was a sept of the Clan Campbell, which is the reason that white and yellow lines are incorporated into the Mackellar tartan. (The tartan itself was registered in 1964, and is based on an early example dating from the 1930s.) 'Mackellar' derives from the Gaelic *Mac Ealair* ('Son of Hilary'), referring to St Hilary of Poitiers (*c.* 315–68), a bishop. Famous MacKellars include the sculptor Archibald McKellar (1884–1901) and the singer Kenneth McKellar (b. 1927).

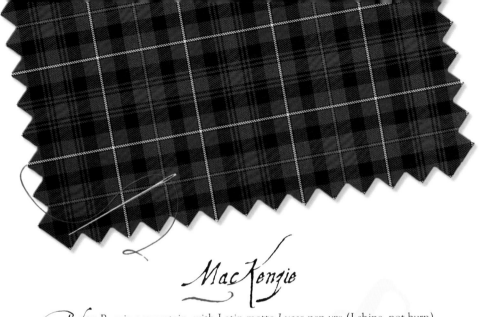

## MacKenzie

**Badge:** Burning mountain, with Latin motto *Luceo non uro* (I shine, not burn)
**Gaelic:** MacCoinnich

Descended from Colin, the 1st Earl of Ross, in the thirteenth century, this clan received the lands of Kintail from David II (r. 1329–71). Despite initial marriage alliances with the MacDonalds, the clans turned against one another, leading to the MacKenzies' crushing victory in the Battle of Blàr na Pàirce in 1491. In the early seventeenth century, the 12th chief, Kenneth, received a charter of the lands of Lochalsh and Lochcarron. MacKenzie fortunes temporarily dipped following the Jacobite rebellion of 1745, but were later restored by service to the crown, including raising the famous Seaforth Highlanders regiment in 1778.

# Mackinlay

*Gaelic:* MacFhionnlaigh (Son of Finlay)

The origins and associations of the Mackinlay clan are historically confused. Traditionally, the clan is held to derive from Findlay, son of Buchanan of Drumikill, but other accounts point to Findlay Mór, the royal standard bearer at the Battle of Pinkie (1547), or key figures in the Farquharsons. The Mackinlay tartan does bear a close resemblance to the Farquharsons, although in balance it is also similar to tartans produced for the MacKenzies, MacLeods and Gordons. The ancestry of the Mackinlays is confused by numerous variant spellings, including Finlay, Finlayson, Donleavy and MacKinley.

## Mackinnon

*Badge:* Boar's head with a deer's shankbone in its mouth, with Latin motto
*Audentes fortuna juvat* (Fortune helps the daring)    *Gaelic:* MacFhionghain

The Mackinnons hail from Mull and Iona, where they served as vassals of the Lords of the Isles, tending to the royal household or providing military commanders for the army. Tradition states that they ultimately derive from Kenneth MacAlpin (*c.* 840–58), son of King Alpin, who ruled Dalriada from 833-41. The Mackinnons were important figures in the life of the monastery on Iona; the clan provided the last abbot there. During both the Civil War and the Jacobite rebellions, the Mackinnons fought in support of the Stuarts, after which their power declined considerably.

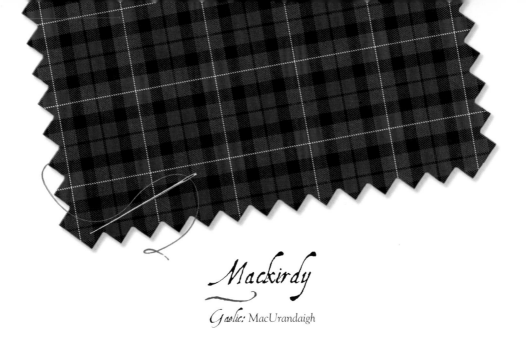

## Mackirdy

*Gaelic:* MacUrandaigh

Recorded history for the Mackirdys begins in the sixteenth century, when a Gilkrist Makurerdy is recorded as living on the Isle of Bute; Mackirdys also inhabited the nearby Isle of Arran. The clan is likely to have been small in stature, the translation of their Gaelic name (Son of the sea king) suggesting that they earned a living from fishing and sailing. (The Gaelic itself may have come from the Viking name Myrkjartan.) The clan is classed as a sept of the Stewarts, who provided the Mackirdys with protection and commercial interaction.

# MacLachlan

**Badge:** Three-towered castle, with Latin motto *Fortis et fides* (Brave and trusty)

**Gaelic:** MacLachlainn

The MacLachlans are of northern Irish descent, settling in Scotland during the thirteenth century in the Loch Fyne area, around Strathlachlan (which became a MacLachlan barony in 1680). Royal charters expanded the clan's landholdings in Argyll during the fourteenth century, and it is noted that a Gillespie MacLachlan was one of those present at the first Scottish parliament, held under Robert the Bruce (r. 1306–29) in 1309. The MacLachlans fought for the Campbells during the seventeenth century and the Stuarts during the eighteenth century, the Jacobite defeat resulting in the destruction of Castle Lachlan.

## MacLaine of Lochbuie

**Badge:** Battle-axe, with branches of laurel and cypress, with Latin motto
*Vincere vel mori* (To conquer or die) **Gaelic:** *MacGillEathain Loch Buidhe*

The motif of this clan relates to Gill-Eathan na Tuaighe – 'Gillean of the battle-axe' – who served Alexander III (r. 1249–86). In reward, Gillean took possession of lands on Mull, and began the clan MacLaine. Later, the clan split into two different branches – the MacLaines of Lochbuie and the MacLeans of Duart. (MacLean was the dominant spelling until the eighteenth century, when the MacLaine spelling became prominent.) The MacLaine of Lochbuie tartan was recorded in the early twentieth century, although the MacLaine of Lochbuie (Coburn) tartan dates back to at least 1810.

## MacLaren

*Badge:* Lion's head, crowned and surrounded by laurel, with Gaelic motto *Creag an Tuirc* ('The Boar's Rock') *Gaelic:* MacLabhrainn

The MacLarens were settled in Strathearn and Balquhidder in Perthshire, and the island of Tiree in Argyllshire, by the late medieval period. They had a turbulent history, fighting with the Campbells and MacGregors, on the side of Robert the Bruce (r. 1306–29) during the independence wars and for the Jacobites in the eighteenth century, the clan nearly meeting its destruction at Culloden. The MacLaren name today is most visible in the McLaren F1 racing team, founded by New Zealander Bruce McLaren in 1963.

## MacLay

*Gaelic:* MacDhuinnShléibhe or Mac an Léigh

The MacLays, or MacLeas, are a widespread clan found in both the Highlands and the Lowlands, and were seen as a sept of the Stewarts of Appin. Regarding origins, one clan tradition has it that the MacLays were descended from someone called Dunsleve. The Lowland MacLays often anglicized their names to 'Livingstone' – hedging its bets, the current clan tartan in registered as 'Livingstone MacLay MacLeay'. The MacLay name begins to appear in records from the early fourteenth century, and later records show that MacLays were often medical practitioners.

## MacLean

**Badge:** Fortified tower, with the motto 'Virtue mine honour'   **Gaelic:** MacGillEathain

The MacLeans trace their origins back to the thunderously titled Gill-Eathan na Tuaighe ('Gillean of the battle-axe'), a thirteenth-century warrior descended from the King of Dalriada. Over time, the MacLeans divided into different family branches, one of the most influential being the MacLeans of Duart, founded by Lachlann Lùbanach (d. *c.* 1405), who became the 5th chief of the MacLean clan. The heavily indebted family lost many of its ancestral lands in strife with the Campbells of Argyll during the 1670s. The MacLean is one of the oldest verified tartans, a hunting pattern that dates back to the late sixteenth century.

## MacLellan

*Badge:* Arm gripping a knife, skewering a moor's head, with the motto 'Think on'
*Gaelic:* MacGillFhaolain

The rather gruesome badge of the MacLellan clan depicts the head of 'Black Morrow', a bandit who was, according to clan tradition, killed by Sir William MacLellan on behalf of King James II (r. 1437–1460). When Sir William presented the bandit's head to the king, James seemed to forget his promises of reward money, provoking the comment 'Think on' from William. The MacLellans were devoted royalists for much of their history, but were without a chief by the nineteenth century, with many MacLellans emigrating to Canada, the United States and Australia.

# MacLeod of Harris

*Badge:* Bull's head framed by flags, with Latin motto *Muros aheneus esto* (Be then a wall of brass) *Gaelic:* MacLeòid na Hearadh

The MacLeod progenitor was the Norse king Leod, son of Olaf the Black (d. *c.* 1237). Olaf ruled over the islands of Man, Lewis, Harris and parts of Skye, plus the North Isles, during the thirteenth century. His seat was at Dunvegan Castle on Skye, and the castle remains the seat of the MacLeod chief to this day, making it one of the oldest continuously occupied castles in British history. The MacLeod of Harris is a senior branch of the MacLeod clan, and is also known as the Sìol Tormoid ('seed of Tormud') after one of Olaf's sons inherited Harris and Dunvegan.

## MacLeod of Lewis

*Badge:* Radiant sun, with Latin motto *Luceo non uro* (I shine, not burn)
*Gaelic:* MacLeòid Leòdhais

Another major strand of the MacLeods, the MacLeods of Lewis are derived from Torquil, brother of the Tormod mentioned in the previous entry. The history of all the branches of the MacLeod clan, including those of Lewis, is largely one of wars and feuding. They were nearly destroyed during the Battle of Worcester in 1651. The Macleod of Lewis tartan is one of the brighter Scottish setts, consisting of black stripes over a yellow background, accented by red stripes. It has even been nicknamed 'Loud MacLeod' on account of its visual volume.

## MacLeod of Raasay

*Badge:* Bull's head framed by flags, with Latin motto *Muros aheneus esto*
(Be then a wall of brass) *Gaelic:* MacGilleChaluim

An offshoot of the MacLeods of Lewis, the MacLeods of Raasay took a royal charter for the lands of Assynt in Sutherland in 1570. The Raasay MacLeods made some notable bad calls throughout their long history. In 1650, the MacLeods sheltered the Marquis of Montrose at Ardveck Castle, following his defeat at the Battle of Philiphaugh (1645). Eventually, the MacLeods betrayed him to the Marquis of Argyll, resulting in his execution and much hostility towards the clan. Support for the Jacobite cause during the eighteenth century also brought much subsequent punishment upon the family.

## MacLintock

*Motto:* Virtute et labore (By valour and hard work)
*Gaelic:* MacGilleFhionndaig ('Son of the servant of St Findon')

We know that, by the sixteenth century, MacLintocks were settled in territories around the western banks of Loch Lomond and throughout Argyll, the name appearing in numerous variants that included MacLinton, MacClinton, MacClintock and MacLlintog. According to which interpretation you follow, the MacLintocks are treated either as a sept of the clan MacDougal or of the clan Colquhoun. The pattern for the MacLintock tartan appears to have originated in the second half of the nineteenth century.

## MacMillan

*Badge:* Two hands gripping a broadsword, with Latin motto *Miseris succerere disco* (I learn to help the unfortunate) *Gaelic:* MacMhaolain or MacGilleMhaoil

The clan MacMillan, as suggested by its Gaelic name (Son of the servant of the tonsured one), probably originated from Celtic monastic communities. We know that a branch of the family was established around Loch Arkaig, Lochaber, during the thirteenth century, and several other branches of the family subsequently emerged and spread widely. From the fourteenth century, one of the most important branches was the MacMillans of Knapdale, who received their lands in 1360 by royal charter from John of Islay (d. 1386), but they also put down roots in Kintyre, Galloway and Kirkcudbrightshire.

## Macnab

**Badge:** Savage's head, with Latin motto *Timor omnis abesto* (Let fear by far from all)
**Gaelic:** Mac an Aba (Son of the abbot)

Another clan with ecclesiastical origins, the Macnabs are descended from hereditary abbots of Glendochart and Strathearn. They were settled around the River Dochart in Perthshire by the eleventh century and grew considerably in power until they allied themselves against Robert the Bruce (r. 1306–29), resulting in a major loss of lands. The Macnabs made peace with the royals during the reign of David II (r. 1329–71), taking the barony of Bovain under royal charter, and later fought for the Royalists during the Civil War and the Jacobites during the Rising of 1745.

# MacNaughton

**Badge:** Embattled castle, with the motto 'I hope in God'
**Gaelic:** MacNeachdainn (Son of the pure one)

Tradition states that the MacNaughtons are descended from one Nachtan Mór – a tenth-century Pictish prince. During the twelfth century, the MacNaughtons settled in Strathtay, having moved from Moray to escape political unrest, and expanded their authority over parts of Loch Awe and Loch Fyne. Opposing Robert the Bruce (r. 1306–29) brought substantial losses in terms of life and landholdings, although David II (r. 1329–71) later granted the clan lands in Lewis. Royalist during the Civil War, the MacNaughtons later fell from grace and their estates were forfeited to the crown in 1691.

## MacNeill

*Badge:* Rock, with the Latin motto *Vincere vel mori* (Conquer or die)    *Gaelic:* MacNéill

The MacNeills have Irish ancestry, being founded by Irish nobles who settled in Barra in the Outer Hebrides in the mid-eleventh century. MacNeill history is soaked in blood. There were two branches of the family – the MacNeills of Barra and the MacNeills of Gigha – and their alliances with other clans meant that on occasions they fought each other. The Barra strand eventually held the chieftainship over all the MacNeills, but the 21st chief, General Roderick MacNeill, was forced to sell Barra in 1838, the lands only returning to MacNeill possession in 1937.

## MacNicol

**Badge:** Demi-lion rampant, with the Latin motto *Generositate (With generosity)*
**Gaelic:** MacNeacail

Descendants of Vikings, the MacNicol lands originally embraced a wide territory in the north-west, taking in Assynt, the Isle of Lewis, and at least part of Skye. Although later displaced by the MacLeods, their name has remained a significant presence in the area. (The synergy between the MacNicols and MacLeods is reflected in a tartan that bears both clan names.) During the seventeenth century, many MacNicols anglicized their names to Nicolson, and indeed the two names became separate clans in 1980.

## MacPhail

*Gaelic:* MacPhàil

The MacPhail name is prevalent throughout Scotland, and emerged during the fifteenth century. Over its history, the name has been found in abundant variations, including MacFall, MacPhael, MacPhayll, Makfele and Makphaile. Depending on interpretation, the MacPhails are regarded as septs of several other clans, including the Camerons, Mackintoshes or the Clan Chattan. At the time of writing, there were four tartans associated with the MacPhails, all of them registered as the clan/family type, and including two hunting types. The designs date from the 1880s to 2002.

## MacPherson

**Badge:** Seated cat, with the motto 'Touch not the cat bot [without] a glove'
**Gaelic:** MacMhuirich or Mac a' Phearsain

The parson referred to in the Gaelic *Mac a' Phearsain* (Son of the parson) is Muireach Cattenach of Kingussie in Badenoch, whose one son and three grandsons founded the MacPherson line. Part of the Clan Chattan – hence the familiar motto – the MacPhersons attempted to take the chieftainship of the confederation, without success. Indeed, over time, the MacPhersons lost many of their lands, either through Jacobite sympathies or through the effects of debt. Despite such losses, there are today numerous tartans associated with the MacPherson name, many of them originating in the nineteenth century.

## MacQuarrie

*Badge:* Mailed arm, emerging from a crown, holding a dagger, with Latin motto *Turris fortis mihi Deus* (God is a tower of strength to me)  *Gaelic:* MacGuaire

The MacQuarrie clan comes from the islands of Mull and Ulva, where they lived from the fifteenth century (the first name on record is one Lord MacQuarrie of Ulva, who signed as witness to a 1463 charter). Supposedly descended from the Sìol Alpin, the MacQuarries were originally vassals of the Lords of the Isles. One notable character from MacQuarrie history is Lachlan MacQuarrie (d. 1818), 16th Lord of Ulva, who played host to Dr Samuel Johnson (1709–84) and James Boswell (1740–95) during their visit to the Hebrides, and lived to the age of 103.

## MacQueen

*Badge:* Wolf holding an arrow, with the motto 'Constant and faithful'
*Gaelic:* MacShuibhne, MacCuinn or MacCuidhein

The MacQueens have a complicated history, the clan developing several branches at different locations. The name itself has a Nordic flavour, meaning 'son of Sweyn', but a focal point for their origins is Argyll, where Suibhne, head of the Castle Sween, ruled in the thirteenth century, but they were also to be found in Skye, Galloway and on the River Findhorn in Inverness-shire. During the fifteenth century, when the clan found itself battling with other clans for power, the MacQueens became part of the Clan Chattan.

## MacRae

*Badge:* Hand holding a sword, with Latin motto *Fortitudine* (With fortitude)
*Gaelic:* MacRath

From the Gaelic meaning 'Son of grace', possibly indicating church associations, the MacRae name traces back to the fourteenth century, when they settled in Kintail in Ross-shire (although the family had earlier connections back to Beauly, Inverness). The MacRaes were noted as warriors, and fought in the service of the MacKenzies of Kintail and at the Battle of Sheriffmuir in 1715. The earliest known date for the tartan's existence is 1850, the pattern being recorded in W. & A. Smith, *Authenticated Tartans of the Clans and Families of Scotland* (1850).

## Mactaggart

*Badge:* Masonic tower, with the motto 'For Commonwealth and Liberty'

*Gaelic:* Mac an t-Sagairt

The Mactaggarts have a particularly spirited progenitor. The Gaelic name *Mac an t-Sagairt* (Son of the priest) refers to Ferquhard Macintaggart, the lay abbot of the monastery of Applecross in *c.* 1215. A rather militaristic man of God, he violently resisted a local rebellion against the authority of Alexander II (r. 1214–49), presenting the king with heads of the rebels. In gratitude, Alexander rewarded him with a knighthood and later made him Earl of Ross (the family is regarded as a sept of the Ross clan).

# MacTavish

*Motto:* Non oblitus (Not forgotten)   *Gaelic:* MacThàmhais

The MacTavishes were, by the twelfth century, established in Dunardarie in Knapdale, Argyll, and were a sept of the nearby Campbells. The Gaelic *Mac Thàmhais* translates as 'Son of Tammas' – a generic rather than specific reference to the Lowland word for the name 'Thomas'. MacTavishes fought primarily for the Jacobite cause during the eighteenth century, the final defeat of the rebellions pushing many clan members abroad to America and Ireland. The anglicized version of the MacTavish name is Thompson.

## MacThomas

*Badge:* Wildcat fighting a snake, with Latin motto *Deo juvante invidiam superabo* (With God's help I will rise above envy) *Gaelic:* MacThòmais

The Clan Chattan produced many different septs and branches, one of which was the Clan MacThomas. The progenitor of the clan was Tòmaidh Mór ('Big Tommy'), great-grandson of the 8th chief of the Clan Chattan Mackintoshes. Tòmaidh lived in the fourteenth century in Inverness-shire but, when the Clan Chattan became too populous, he moved his people to Glee Shee, Perthshire, and began a distinct MacThomas (also McComie) line. The clan had a complicated relationship with royalty during the Civil War years, and lost much land in 1676, before moving to places such as Angus and Fife.

## MacWhirter

*Gaelic: Mac a' Chruiteir*

The MacWhirter name was made famous to several generations of British children by the writer and television presenter Norris MacWhirter (1925–2004), who, with his brother Ross (1925–75), founded the *Guinness Book of Records*. Norris also co-presented the BBC 'Record Breakers' television show. The MacWhirter name means 'Son of the harper', referring to the court musicians that were common in royal and noble households. The MacWhirters are specifically descended from the royal harpers who were granted the estate of Dalelachane in the fourteenth century.

# MacWilliam

*Gaelic:* MacUilleim

This Highland clan has a particularly dark early history. The progenitor of the clan was William, the illegitimate son of Duncan II (r. 1094) – Duncan was murdered in November 1094 after less than a year of rule. The kindred established its own chiefs – indeed, claimants of the Scottish throne – until 1215, when the baby daughter and only surviving heir of the clan chief was killed, beaten to death against the market cross in Forfar. This terrible event was not the end of the MacWilliam line, as other branches continued elsewhere, becoming septs of the MacFarlanes, MacPhersons and Gunns.

## Maitland

*Badge:* Lion sejant holding a sword, with Latin motto *Consilio et animis*
(By counsel and reasoning)

The motto of the Maitland clan reflects the role that generations of Maitlands held in matters of state. Originating in the Lowlands at least as early as the twelfth century, the Maitlands provided many key officials in royal households. These included Sir John Maitland (1537–95), Lord Chancellor and Secretary of Scotland, and another John Maitland (1616–82), the 2nd Earl (later 1st Duke) of Lauderdale, who became Secretary of State, Governor of Edinburgh Castle and Lord High Commissioner to Parliament.

# Malcolm

**Badge:** Silver tower, with Latin motto *In ardua petit* (He aims at difficult things)
**Gaelic:** MacCaluim

One problem with unpacking the history of the Malcolms is that Malcolm and MacCallum were often used interchangeably. Some clarity was obtained in 1779, when the MacCallums took the estate of Poltalloch and changed their name to Malcolm. (An heir, the politician John Wingfield Malcolm of Poltalloch, was created Lord Malcolm in 1896.) The name actually means 'Son of the followers of St Columba' (*c.* 521–97); the saint was energetic in diffusing Christianity throughout Scotland during the sixth century. The Malcolms produced many great military leaders during the eighteenth and nineteenth centuries.

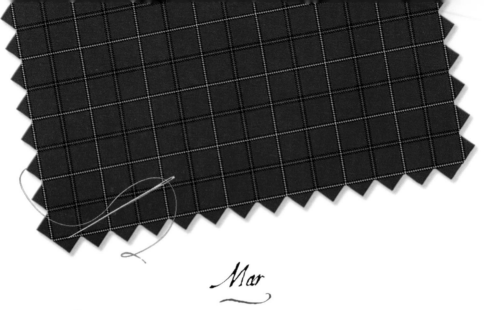

## Mar

*Badge:* Ten feathers on a cap, with phonetic French motto *Pans plus* (Think more)
*Gaelic:* Màr

The name has a geographical origin, referring to the Mar region in Aberdeenshire. In ancient Scotland, Mar was ruled by a *mormaer* (steward) and, in time, this position evolved into the Earl of Mar. The first Earl of Mar was Rothri (d. *c.* 1141), and the position became a highly influential one in Scotland – Isabella of Mar (1277–96) married Robert the Bruce (r. 1306–29) in 1295, and later marital associations connected the Mars with the Stuarts. Royal connections were affected in the eighteenth century, however, when John Erskine (1675–1732) led the Jacobite Rebellion of 1715.

# Matheson

**Badge:** Arm holding a sword, with Latin motto *Fac et spera* (Do and hope)
**Gaelic:** MacMhathain

The Mathesons' Gaelic name translates as 'Son of a bear' or 'Son of a hero'. Tradition claims that the clan is descended from a twelfth-century noble called Gilleoin, who helped overthrow the Picts during the ninth century. Historically, we know that, by the late medieval period, the Mathesons had settled around Lochalsh and Shinness, these settlements forming two distinct branches of the family. During the nineteenth century, several Matheson figures went on to become leading international figures in finance and commerce.

## Maxwell

*Badge:* Stag standing in front of a holly bush, with Latin motto *Reviresco* (I grow strong again)

The tartan of the Maxwell clan dates back to 1842, when it was recorded in the *Vestiarium Scoticum*. There are several other Maxwell tartans, including one developed for the US Clan Maxwell Society in the 1980s. Of Norman origins, the Maxwell clan established itself in Scotland during the twelfth century. Early records of Maxwells include Sir John Maxwell (d. 1241), the Chamberlain of Scotland, and Sir Herbert Maxwell, a signatory on the Ragman Rolls. Much later Maxwells of note include the physicist James Clerk Maxwell (1831–79).

## Melville

The Melville name is of Norman derivation, taken from the barony of Malaville or Malleville in the Pays de Caux in Normandy. The de Malleville family came to Scotland in the early twelfth century with the returning King David I (r. 1124–53), and continued to exercise influence for many centuries to come, but particularly during the reigns of James V (r. 1513–42) and Mary, Queen of Scots (r. 1542–57). It should be noted that the Melvilles use two mottoes: the one above, and *Pro rege et patria* ('For king and country').

## Menzies

*Badge:* The head of a savage, with the motto 'With God I shall' *Gaelic:* Meinnearach

The Menzies name derives from the town of Mesnières, near Rouen. During the twelfth century, members of the de Meyneris family settled in Scotland, and one Robert de Meyneris is recorded as chamberlain to Alexander II (r. 1214–49). In the wars of Scottish independence, the Menzies sided with Robert the Bruce (r. 1306–29), for which they were rewarded with lands in Glendochart and Glenlochry. Later, they fought for the royalists during the Civil War and for the Jacobites during the Rebellions. One noteworthy Menzies contribution to the Scottish environment was the introduction of the larch and monkey-puzzle trees in the eighteenth century.

## Merrilees

The Merrilees tartan is a curiosity because it began as a nineteenth-century fashion sett, based on literary references, and then eventually became a family tartan. It was registered in 1842 and was named after Meg Merrilees, the gypsy heroine of Sir Walter Scott's romance novel *Guy Mannering* (1815). The novel was extremely popular, and the resourceful Merrilees character captured Scottish public imagination but, over time, the fictional reference was lost and the tartan was adopted by people with the surname Merrilees. The tartan itself is an inversion of the Dress MacPherson design.

## Middleton

*M*iddleton family history appears to begin in the eleventh century, when the estate of Middleton near Laurencekirk, Kincardineshire, was established by King Duncan II (r. 1294). Middletons appear in several official contexts over subsequent centuries, including a signatory to the Ragman Rolls in 1296. During the seventeenth and eighteenth centuries, the Middletons vacillated in their support for Royalists, Covenanters and Jacobites, support for the last resulting in the loss of the earldom of Middleton. A notable Middleton was Thomas Middleton (1570–1627), the famous Jacobean playwright.

## Moffat

*Badge:* Crest coronet with a cross-crosslet, with Latin motto *Spero meliora*
(Hope for better things)

The Clan Moffat has had a rather interrupted history. Dating back to the eleventh century, it hailed from Upper Annandale in Dumfriesshire, taking its name from the town of Moffat. Throughout its history, the clan seems to have had strong church associations: a Nicholas de Mufet is named as Archdeacon of Teviotdale in 1245, and the clan later produced missionaries, church treasurers and theologians. Yet the clan's chieftainship suffered a long hiatus following the death of the incumbent chief in the 1560s. Only in 1983 was a new chief finally appointed.

## Moncreiffe

*Badge:* Demi-lion issuing from a coronet, with French motto *Sur esperance* (Upon hope)

*Gaelic:* Mon Chraoibh

The original Gaelic name of the clan, *Mon* or *Monadh Chraoibh*, means 'Hill of the [sacred] tree' and refers to a hill in its Perthshire barony that was used as a place of worship by the Picts. Moncreiffe clan histories vary in accounts of origins. The most popular version is that the Moncreiffes descended from Pictish royalty, while others claim that the Moncreiffes are of Anglo-Norman origins. The name appears in an official context during the thirteenth century, when a document refers to Alexander II (r. 1214–49) granting Matthew de Moncreiffe the lands of Moncreiffe by royal charter.

# Montgomery

**Badge:** Female figure holding an anchor in one hand and a savage's head in the other, with French motto *Gardez bien* (Look well)  **Gaelic:** MacGumaraid

The Montgomery name, in modern times, is primarily associated with the British Army soldier Field Marshal Bernard Montgomery (1887–1976), the 1st Viscount Montgomery of Alamein, famed for his command of British troops in the Second World War. Another famous military ancestor was Richard Montgomery (1738–75), an Irish-born leader who fought in various North American wars. The Montgomerys were originally Norman settlers, the clan progenitor being Roger de Montgomery, regent of Normandy. After settling in Scotland, the clan acquired lands throughout Renfrewshire and Ayrshire.

## Morrison

*Badge:* Arm, gripping a dagger, issuing from a tower atop waves, with the motto
*Dun Eistein* (Castle Eistein)   *Gaelic:* MacGilleMhoire

By legend descended from a Norse family shipwrecked off the coast of Lewis – the badge refers to the family's journey ashore – the Morrisons were settled on Lewis by the eleventh century. There, the Morrisons of Habost took the office of *brieve* (judge), which they held on a hereditary basis until the seventeenth century. Around this time, conflict with the MacLeods pushed many of the Lewis Morrisons over to the mainland and other islands, and today, there are several branches of the Morrison clan across Scotland. The Morrison clan tartan is based on references stretching back to 1747.

## Mowat

*Badge:* Man in armour holding a sword and flag atop a castellated tower,
with Latin motto *Monte alto* (High mount)

The Mowat clan dates back to the first half of the twelfth century, the first recorded ancestor being Robert Montealto, a Norman knight (although the name suggests Italian as much as Norman origins). Montealto had originally held lands in North Wales, but settled in Scotland during the reign of David I (r. 1124–53). The Mowats subsequently settled widely across Scotland, with estates in Caithness, Aberdeenshire, Angus, Ayrshire and the Shetlands. The earliest reference to a Mowat clan tartan was in the *Clans Originaux*, published in Paris in 1880 by J. Claude Fres Et Cie.

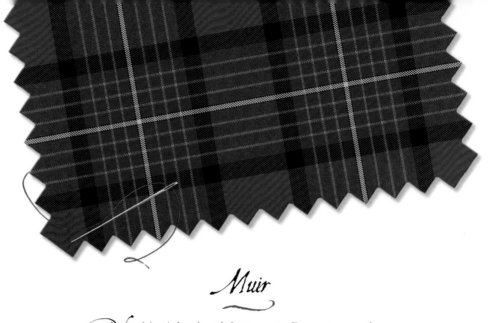

## Muir

*Badge:* Moor's head, with Latin motto *Durum patientia frango*
(I overcome difficulties with patience) *Gaelic:* Moire or Mór

From the thirteenth century, there is a reference to one Gilchrist Mure, who fought at the Battle of Largs in 1263. Gilchrist is the earliest reference to an ancestor of the Muirs, but the name appears frequently thereafter in official records. Sir Archibald Muir, for example, helped defend Berwick from the assault of Edward I (r. 1272–1307) in 1296, and died in the process, while his son William was knighted by David II (r. 1329–71). In 1346, Elizabeth Muir married the future Robert II (r. 1371–90), the couple producing the later King Robert III (r. 1390–1406).

## Munro

*Badge:* Spread eagle, with the motto 'Dread God'   *Gaelic:* Mac an Rothaich

A martial clan, the original Ross-shire settlers may well have been mercenary soldiers employed by the Earl of Ross to fight the Vikings. Over the next two centuries, the Munros increased their landholdings on the north side of the Cromarty Firth, and fought hard against the English. In this they suffered, losing large numbers of the men and their chief at the Battle of Pinkie (1547) and enduring the destruction of their seat, Foulis Castle, during the Jacobite Rebellion of 1745. The most prominent Monro in history is James Munro (1758–1831), the fifth President of the United States.

## Murray

*Badge:* Mermaid holding a mirror, with the French motto *Tout prêt* (Quite ready)
*Gaelic:* Moireach

Descended from Flemish noble stock who settled in Scotland during the twelfth century, the Murrays are one of the most influential clans in all of Scottish history. The progenitor was Freskin de Moravia, who was granted the territory of Moireabh (Moray) by David I (r. 1124–53). The family subsequently grew powerful and extensive, spreading out across Scotland and forming several major branches, such as the Murrays of Bothwell, Tullibardine (*see* page 252) and Atholl (*see* page 251). There are currently 23 tartans bearing the Murray name, most dating from the nineteenth and twentieth centuries.

## Murray of Atholl

*Badge:* Demi-savage holding a dagger and a key, with the motto 'Furth fortune and fill the fetters' (Go forth, seek fortune, and return with wealth)   *Gaelic:* Moireach Athall

The Murrays of Atholl are the most prominent branch of the Clan Atholl. The line began with the marriage of the 2nd Earl of Tullibardine, William Murray, to the daughter of the Earl of Atholl in 1629. By the beginning of the eighteenth century, the then Marquess of Atholl was made a Duke, reflecting his political power at the time. Today, the Duke of Atholl controls the only legal private (although purely ceremonial) army in Europe, the Atholl Highlanders, formed in the eighteenth century to fight in the American War of Independence.

# Murray of Tullibardine

*Badge:* Demi-savage holding a dagger and a key, with the motto 'Furth fortune and fill the fetters' (Go forth, seek fortune, and return with wealth)  *Gaelic:* Moireach Thulach Bàrdainn

The Murrays of Tullibardine are descended from a grandson of Freskin de Moravia, William, who acquired by marriage the lands of Tullibardine. The lands became a barony in 1443, and the family was influential in the Scottish court. One of the most powerful early figures of this line was Sir John Murray (1550–1614), the 12th Lord, who became a leading figure in James VI's court and subsequently Lord Murray (1604) and the Earl of Tullibardine (1606). The Murrays of Tullibardine have several tartans, a number of which date back to the seventeenth century.

## Napier

*Badge:* Hand grasping an eagle's leg, with Latin motto *Vincit veritas* (Truth prevails)

The Napier name is a forceful presence in British history. The earliest reference, in the thirteenth century, is to one John de Napier of Dumbartonshire. Over the next few centuries, the Napiers established themselves in the Scottish and British royal courts, and rose high in civic service – Alexander Napier (d. 1454) was Provost of Edinburgh, and his son Alexander (d. *c.* 1475) was Vice Admiral of Scotland. Subsequent Napier luminaries include mathematician John Napier (1550–1617), army commander Sir Charles Napier (1782–1853) and shipbuilder Robert Napier (1791–1876).

# Nesbitt

*Badge:* Black boar, with the motto 'I byde it'

Berwickshire is the ancestral homeland of the Nesbitts, the name deriving from the hamlets of East and West Nisbet. ('Nisbet' is a variant spelling of 'Nesbitt', although the latter was probably more common until the sixteenth century.) The Nesbitt name begins appearing on civic records prior to the Norman Conquest, and it also features on the Ragman Rolls of 1296. During the sixteenth century, the Nesbitts varied in their allegiances, some fighting for the Royalists and being rewarded with peerages, while others opted to support the Covenanters.

## Ogilvie

**Badge:** Woman holding a portcullis, with French motto *Á fin* (To the end)
**Gaelic:** MacGilleBhuidhe

The Ogilvies are descended from Gilbert, born of the Earl of Angus, who received the barony of Ogilvie, Forfarshire, from William I the Lion (r. 1165–1214). Gilbert's descendants went on to do well for themselves, serving as hereditary sheriffs of Angus and acquiring further baronies. In 1491, Sir John Ogilvy of Lintrathern received Airlie Castle by royal charter, although this was subsequently destroyed during the Civil War. There are today many Ogilvie tartans, some being the most complex of modern sets in terms of design and weaving.

## Oliphant

*Badge:* Gold crescent, with the motto 'What was may be'

The Oliphants are descended from David de Olifard, a Norman knight who was part of the retinue of King David I (r. 1124–53). Having been granted Roxburghshire lands in the twelfth century, the Oliphants secured their positions through judicious marriages, gaining the peerage of lord in the mid-fifteenth century. In later history, the Oliphants suffered on account of their support for the Jacobites. The name is also closely associated with the Melville family; the two families share the same tartan, which was first recorded in 1842.

# Paisley

*Badge:* Abbot flanked by cinquefoils, with the motto 'Lord, let Paisley flourish by the preaching of thy word'  *Gaelic:* Pàislig

Located in the west-central Lowlands of Scotland, the town of Paisley grew from a monastic community established there in the sixth or seventh century (the Romans may have also had a fort in the area). In the fifteenth century, the burgh of Paisley became a barony, and the town steadily gained a reputation for its skills in weaving (which produced the well-known Paisley pattern) and also for its artistic and literary communities. Today, it is the biggest town in Scotland, and its district tartan was designed by Allan C. Drennan in 1952.

# Perthshire

*Badge:* Highlander with a claymore and targe, with Latin motto
*Pro lege et libertate* (For law and liberty)   *Gaelic:* Siorrachd Pheairt

The Perthshire district tartan originates in a design that dates back to 1831 and was recorded by Wilsons of Bannockburn as 'Perthshire Rock and Wheel' (the 'Rock and Wheel' refers to a soft type of tartan). Located in central Scotland, Perthshire's positioning has given it an equally central place in Scottish history, as testified by the large number of stately homes and fortifications that dot the landscape. More primitive Stone Age and Iron Age settlements are also common, and the Romans later placed several garrisons in the region.

# Pride of Scotland

*Gaelic:* Àrdan na h-Alba

The 'Pride of Scotland' label has been applied to a wide variety of contemporary tartans, most registered in the late twentieth and early twenty-first centuries. On the Scottish Register of Tartans, all of these designs are registered as 'Fashion' varieties, serving to evoke a general sense of Scottish pride rather than target a specific clan or individual. In this way, the Pride of Scotland designs are often used by kilt hire shops to target those with no specific clan connections, or a need for a uniform appearance. Many of the Pride of Scotland designs have been designed by McCalls of Aberdeen, a major modern tartan maker.

# Prince of Wales

*Gaelic:* Prionnsa na Cuimrigh

The Prince of Wales tartan was designed in 1998 by Lochcarron of Galashiels. It was originally intended to be part of the Duke of Rothesay collection, a title held by the Prince of Wales, as the heir apparent to the throne of the United Kingdom. A mistake in the patterning, however, led to this tartan being called simply 'Prince of Wales'. To reflect the Prince's full title, the tartan makes use of the red, white and green colours associated with the Welsh flag. Although the flag's iconography dates back to at least the medieval period, and possibly as far back as Roman times, it was only officially adopted by the Welsh nation in 1959.

# Raeburn

**Badge:** Stag's head, with Latin motto *Tutis fortis* (Safe if strong)

The Raeburn name derives from the Ayrshire village of Ryburn in the parish of Dunlop. As a surname, Raeburn became widely diffused across Scotland in several varieties, including Reburne and Raburn. The earliest recorded ancestor was William of Raeburn, who acted as a witness on a document in 1331, and one Andrew de Raburn, who was burgess of Glasgow in 1430. Sir Henry Raeburn (1756–1823) became one of Scotland's most famous portrait painters. During the early nineteenth century, he recorded many tartans in his artwork, a valuable record for tartan researchers.

# Ramsay

**Badge:** Unicorn's head, with Latin motto *Ora et labora* (Pray and work)

Of Anglo-Norman ancestry, the Ramsays' earliest recorded historical figure is Sir Symon de Ramsay, a knight who was given lands in Lothian by David I (r. 1124–53). Although the Ramsay name was on the Ragman Rolls of 1296, the clan later supported Robert the Bruce (r. 1306–29), and they contributed significantly to the Wars of Independence. The Ramsays of Dalhousie, one of the most prominent lines of the clan, were in favour with the British royals during the seventeenth century, being raised to the peerage, and Ramsays subsequently played significant roles in national and colonial service.

## Rangers F.C.

The Rangers Football Club, with its home currently in the Ibrox stadium in south-west Glasgow, is as much known for the passion of its fans as the quality of its play. Unsurprisingly, therefore, there are several corporate tartans related to the club. The first of the contemporary range was designed in 1989 by Messrs John MacGregor of Glasgow, the player Ally McCoist showing off the tartan by wearing full Highland dress at the opening game of the season in September. A variant of the sett was designed in 1994 by Chris Aitken of Geoffrey (Tailor) Highland Crafts, to match the club colours, and his design is the basis of the current club tartan.

## Rankin

**Badge:** Cubit arm holding a battle-axe  **Gaelic:** MacFhraing

Today, Rankin is a name rather than a clan, although originally the Rankins were a sept of the MacLeans. The Rankins' origins were as hereditary pipers to various branches of the MacLean clan, and they maintained their reputation as pipers well into the eighteenth century. The earliest known reference to a Rankin is on a document dating back to 1504. Although the Rankins dispersed, the family gave its name to the Ayrshire village of Rankinston. Famous Rankins of recent generations include the scientist Sir William Rankine (1820–75) and the novelist Ian Rankin (b. 1960).

# Rattray

**Badge:** Heart surmounting a five-pointed star rising out of a coronet, with Latin motto *Super sidera votum* (A desire beyond the stars)  **Gaelic:** *Raitear*

The Rattrays are descended from a thirteenth-century knight called Alan de Rateriffe (d. 1210), who received a knighthood from James IV (r. 1488–1513) in the first year of the king's reign. The ancestral seat is Rattray Castle, but this building passed into the ownership of the Earl of Atholl during the sixteenth century, and the Rattrays were forced to move to Craighall Castle near the River Ericht. Rattray history is bloody, with many of its chiefs and leaders either dying in battle or being murdered, although the estates came back into family hands in 1648.

## Rennie

The Rennie name is found across Scotland and dates back to the Middle Ages. There is no ancestral seat as such, although Kilrenny in Fife, formerly a royal burgh, alludes to a concentration of the Rennie family. Variations of the name include Rainy and Rainnie, and the family has often been regarded as a sept of the MacDonnells of Keppoch. Famous Rennies include Charles Rennie Mackintosh (1868–1933) – Rennie being his mother's maiden name – who has a tartan in his honour, designed by Charles Randak in July 2009. There is also a personal Rennie tartan dating from 1980 and designed for Robin Rennie of Fife.

# Robertson

**Badge:** Hand holding a crown, with Latin motto *Virtutis gloria merces* (Glory is the reward of valour) **Gaelic:** MacDhonnchaidh

The Robertsons are descended from Donnachadh Reamhar (Stout Duncan), an ally of Robert the Bruce (r. 1306–29), whose name is apparent in the Gaelic *MacDhonnchaidh*. The Clan Dhonnachaidh was transformed into Robertson by the fortunes of Robert Riabhach ('Riabhach' meaning 'grizzled'), who received the barony of Struan by royal charter in 1451, for his part in capturing the assassins of James I (r. 1406–37). The history of the Robertsons is replete with martial feats and figures, the clan fighting for the Stuarts in the seventeenth and eighteenth centuries.

# Robertson of Kindeace

**Badge:** Hand holding a crown, with Latin motto *Virtutis gloria merces*
(Glory is the reward of valour) **Gaelic:** *MacDhonnachaidh Chinn Déis*

The power of the Robertsons ensured that they spawned several branches, of which the Robertsons of Kindeace is one. The tartan was first recorded in the early nineteenth century, as part of the Cockburn Collection. Now held in the Mitchell Library in Glasgow, the collection has some of the oldest surviving tartan specimens. This tartan is also known as 'Hunting Robertson'. The Scottish Register of Tartans notes that 'The sett is reputedly ancient, and resembles the "Athol Murray", though used only by the Robertsons of the North.'

# Rollo

**Badge:** Stag's head, with French motto *La fortune passé partout*
(Fortune makes way through everything)

The Rollo clan have a dramatic ancestry stretching all the way back to the Viking age. The Rollo Vikings, such as Sigurd and his son Einar, were Nordic raiders who attacked not only the Scottish coastline but also that of Normandy. The tribe's descendants eventually put down roots in Normandy, where they became dukes. In 1066, some of those dukes came to Britain, and settled in Scotland following David I's claiming of the Scottish throne in 1124. Thus the Rollo clan was established, the clan receiving estates at Duncrub that eventually became a barony.

## Rose

*Badge:* Harp, with the motto 'Constant and true'  *Gaelic:* Ròs

The Rose family moved from England to Scotland, settling in Nairn in the twelfth century, their ultimate origins lying in the French village of Ros in Normandy. The main seat of the Rose family was, and remains, Kilravock Castle, built on lands acquired by the family in the late thirteenth century. The castle has played host to great figures from Scotland's past. In addition to Mary, Queen of Scots (r. 1542–57) and James VI (r. 1567–1625), Bonnie Prince Charlie (1720–88) stayed there just before the Battle of Culloden in 1745.

# Ross

**Badge:** Hand holding a laurel crown, with Latin motto
*Spem successus alit* (Success feeds hope) **Gaelic:** Ros

The Ross clan are descended from the Celtic chief Fearchar Mac-an-t-sagairt of Applecross, who lived during the twelfth/thirteenth century and was appointed the Earl of Ross by Alexander II (r. 1214–49) in c. 1234. The earldom lasted until 1372, when the incumbent earl died without an heir. Many of the Ross family were transported out to America after they allied themselves with Charles I (r. 1625–49) during the Civil War, suffering a heavy defeat at the Battle of Worcester in 1651. The present Ross tartan is that recorded in the Cockburn Collection of 1810–20.

## Rothesay

**Badge:** Galley, triple-towered castle, crescent and tenny star on one side and a fess chequy on the other **Gaelic:** Baile Bhòid

The Rothesay tartan is a district sett, celebrating the town of Rothesay on the Isle of Bute. During the nineteenth century, Bute became a major holiday destination, drawing in tourists (particularly from Glasgow) with features such as an electric tram and music halls. The Rothesay tartan ranks alongside seven other tartans with Rothesay in the title. They date from between the early 1800s and the early 2000s, and include three royal setts – as noted above (*see* page 26), the position of Duke of Rothesay is held by the heir apparent to the British throne.

# Roy, Rob

*Gaelic:* Rob Ruadh

Rob Roy MacGregor (1671–1734) is a figure both legendary and ambiguous in Scottish history. Born on the banks of Lake Katrine in Stirlingshire, he developed a career as a cattle rustler, also running cattle 'protection rackets', thereby extorting money from local farmers to ensure the safety of their herds. Yet he also momentarily rose to greatness, fighting vigorously for the Jacobite cause and distinguishing himself at the Battle of Killiecrankie on 27 July 1689. The 'Rob Roy' tartan was designed for Sir John MacGregor Murray of MacGregor (1785–1841), and is apparently based upon tartans worn by Rob Roy, seen in portraits dating back to 1704.

## Royal and Ancient

*Gaelic:* Rìoghail is Àrsaidh

The Royal and Ancient tartan is a corporate sett designed specifically for the Royal and Ancient Golf Club at St Andrews, one of the world's finest golf courses and scene of major international competitions. The 'Ancient' part of the club's name is fully warranted – the club was founded in 1754 – and it also played (and still plays) a central role in codifying the rules of golf. Championships held at the ground include the Open Championship and the Walker Cup, two of the biggest events in the golfing calendar. This tartan was designed in 1993 by Kinlock Anderson Ltd, and proceeds from its sale were used to raise money for building restoration projects.

## Royal Stewart

*Badge:* Seated lion holding a sword and sceptre, with the motto 'In defens'
*Gaelic:* Stiùbhartach Rìoghail

As the name suggests, the Royal Stewart/Stuart tartan is the official tartan of the British royal family, and it is also worn by pipers of certain royal British Army regiments, such as the Royal Scots Dragoon Guards and the Scots Guards. However, unlike exclusive setts such as the Balmoral tartan (*see* page 27), the Royal Stewart tartan can be worn by all the Queen's subjects. This permissive policy has produced some ironic fashions – during the 1970s, for example, punk rockers were often seen wearing Royal Stewart tartan, making an iconoclastic statement.

## Ruthven

*Badge:* Ram's head, with Scots motto *Deid schaw* (Deeds show)  *Gaelic:* Ruadhainn

The Clan Ruthven probably takes its name from the lands of Ruthven, Angus, where Norse chief Sweyn Thorsson settled during the eleventh century. In 1488, William of Ruthven (d. 1513) was made a lord, but the Ruthvens' subsequent behaviour was often at odds with the establishment. Patrick, the 3rd Lord of Ruthven (c. 1520–66) helped in 1566 with the murder of David Rizzio (c. 1533–66), the secretary of Mary, Queen of Scots, and Ruthvens were also involved in the kidnapping of James VI (r. 1567–1625). The Ruthven name was banned and their estates confiscated, restoration not coming until the 1930s.

# St Andrews

**Badge:** St Andrew and his saltire cross on one side, and a boar and an oak tree on the other, with Latin motto *Dum spiro spero* (While I breathe, I hope)  **Gaelic:** *Cill Rimhinn*

St Andrews is not only home to the prestigious Royal and Ancient golf course (*see* page 274), but is also the location for one of Britain's most venerable and respected universities (and Scotland's first), established during the early fifteenth century. The town, nestled on the east coast of Scotland in Fife, has ecclesiastical origins, the name deriving from the building of a shrine to St Andrew in the fourth century. Although the university has its own tartan, designed in the 1990s, the tartan shown here is the district sett, created during the 1930s.

# St Columba

*Gaelic:* Calum Cille

St Columba (*c.* 521–97) is a landmark figure in the history of British spirituality. Born in Ireland, he founded two monasteries in his native country before moving to Scotland, and there founded the great monastery on Iona in the 560s. Iona thus became central to the spread of Christianity throughout Scotland and further afield, and to this day remains a popular place for both tourism and pilgrimage. The tartan was designed in 1996, using colours native to the environment, the proceeds of sales going towards the restoration of a church roof.

# Scotland 2000

### Gaelic: Alba 2000

T he millennium celebrations in 2000 inspired a huge wave of national enthusiasm and fervour across the United Kingdom. Throughout Scotland, not only were there celebrations in every town and city, but also many clans expressed pride in their history through individual events. The Scotland 2000 tartan was a 1998 commission, designed by Arthur MacKie of the Strathmore Woollen Company in Forfar. It was intended purely as a commemorative tartan, based on traditional Scottish colours and able to be worn by all. During and since the millennium, the tartan has been a useful sett to decorate all manner of goods, from teddy bears to mugs, as well as being used in clothing.

# Scott

**Badge:** Stag, with Latin motto Amo (I love)    **Gaelic:** Scotach

The progenitor of the Scott clan was Uchtredus Filius Scoti, a noble figure of the Border regions, whose name appears on a charter dated 1120. Uchtredus had two sons, who created the two main branches of the Scott family: the Scotts of Buccleuch and the Scotts of Balweary. Both branches were influential and powerful, although today, only the Scotts of Buccleuch remain, the line of the Scotts of Balweary coming to an end in 1902. The most famous Scotts are the explorer Captain Robert Scott (1868–1912) and writer Sir Walter Scott (1771–1832).

# Scott (Red)

*Badge:* Harp, with the motto 'Constant and true'  *Gaelic:* Scotach (Dearg)

Sir Walter Scott's position in the history of Scottish identity (*see* Introduction and next entry) has ensured the creation of numerous tartans in his honour, both during his life and after. The design seen here is first referenced in 1829, when Sir Thomas Dick Lauder (1784–1848) wrote to Scott saying, according to the Scottish Register of Tartans, 'that he had seen this tartan in a manuscript prepared for the brothers John Sobieski Stuart and Charles Edward Stuart. Scott rejected the idea very firmly.' Despite this rejection, the Scott (Red) has become one of the most popular of a large number of Scott setts.

# Scott, Sir Walter

**Badge:** Nymph holding the sun and the moon, with Latin motto
*Reparabit cornua Phoebe* (Phoebe will restore courage)

Sir Walter Scott (1771–1832) was a poet and novelist, born in Edinburgh in 1871. By the 1820s, he was one of Britain's most popular writers, primarily on the basis of his fiction rather than his poetry. He also did much to refine a sense of Scottish national identity. Scott struggled desperately at times with his finances, facing ruin on at least two occasions. Yet he rose to become a royal favourite because of his ostentatious preparations for George IV's official visit to Edinburgh in 1822.

## Scottish Knights Templar

The origins of the Knights Templar reach back to twelfth-century France, when they were founded as a monastic order dedicated to the protection of pilgrims going to and from the Holy Land. (Many pilgrims were killed by bandits while passing through the Crusader states to Jerusalem.) The Templars grew to be a politically and militarily powerful order, but were crushed in the fourteenth century by the Catholic Church. Before that event, the Templars had established themselves in Scotland, and a recent revival of the name as an aid organization led to the creation of three distinctive tartans by Stuart Davidson in 1998.

# Scrymgeour

*Badge:* Mantled hand holding a sabre, with Latin motto *Dissipate* (Scatter)

The Clan Scrymgeour was established in Scotland by the end of the thirteenth century. At first settling around Fife, the Scrymgeours became principally known for their presence around Dundee – in 1298, one Alexander Scrymgeour was appointed as the Constable of Dundee Castle, the first of a long hereditary line, and in 1660, John Scrymgeour (d. 1668) became the Earl of Dundee. When he died, the Scrymgeour lands were seized by the Duke of Lauderdale, and they were not restored to the clan until 1954. The name itself comes from the Old English word *skrymsher*, meaning 'swordsman'.

## Sempill

*Badge:* Stag's head

While the origins of the Sempill clan are uncertain (the Norman town of St Pol is a possibility), they were settled in Renfrewshire during the twelfth century. The earliest recorded ancestor is Robert de Sempill (*fl. c.* 1280), who held the position of hereditary sheriff of Renfrew. The clan went on to spill much blood in the cause of Scottish independence but, despite its past opposition to the English crown, the peerage of Lord Sempill has continued to this day, the current lord being the 21st.

## Seton

The Seton clan dates to the twelfth century; an Alexander de Seton signed a charter as witness in 1150. The name comes, according to modern theories, from either the village of Sai in Normandy or the Scottish town of Tranent, owned by the Setons whose name translates as 'sea town'. The position of Lord of Seton and Tranent was bestowed upon the Seton chief during the reign of James I (r. 1406–37). There are currently two Seton tartans, the tartan seen here, which was first recorded in 1842, and a hunting variant from the 1930s.

## Shaw

The Shaws were a powerful component of the Clan Chattan, descended from Shaw Bucktooth, the great-grandson of the 6th chief of the Mackintoshes. Bucktooth distinguished himself fighting for the Clan Chattan. He was rewarded with the lands of Rothiemurchus in 1396, and subsequent generations proved equally warlike, fighting in wars throughout the fifteenth, sixteenth and seventeenth centuries. The Shaw clan tartan dates back to a publication of 1845, which showed a kilted representation of Farquhar Shaw of the Black Watch, who was executed for mutiny in 1743.

## Sinclair

Of Norman ancestry (the name derives from the village of Saint-Clair-sur-Epte), the Clan Sinclair's ancestor is one William de St Clair, an eleventh-century noble who held the barony of Roslin in Midlothian. Sinclairs proved themselves to be great military leaders. Sir Henry Sinclair (1060–1110) was at the head of a victorious Scottish attack on Alnwick Castle in 1093, and another Sir Henry (1100–65) was critical in pulling Northumberland back under Scottish authority. Subsequent Sinclair battle honours read like a history of British wars, from Bannockburn in 1314 to colonial wars in North America in the eighteenth century.

## Skene

**Badge:** Arm issuing from a cloud, holding a laurel crown, with Latin motto
*Virtutis regia merces* (A palace is the reward of valour) **Gaelic:** *Sgainn*

The Skene tartan's origins are complicated. This sett, however, was established during the nineteenth century, and today is one of seven different Skene tartans. Traditionally, the Skene clan is held to have descended from one Struan Robertson, who, during the eleventh century, saved the king by killing a wolf, and was granted the lands of Skene, Aberdeenshire, in recognition of his service. Note also that some historians believe the Skenes to be a sept of the Clan Donnchaidh, before it became the Clan Robertson.

# Spens

*Badge:* Stag's head, with Latin motto *Si deus quis contra?* (If God is present, who is against?)

The Spens clan claims a descent from the ancient Earls of Fife; they certainly enjoyed the protection of the earls for over one hundred years. We have a record of a Henry de Spens of Lathallan, Fife, who lived during the late thirteenth century and who swore his allegiance to Edward I (r. 1272–1307) in 1296, and, during the fifteenth century, the Spens lands were granted as a barony. The surname Spens also related to the royal position of keeper of the larder, seen in English names such as Spenser and Spencer.

## Stevenson

The Stevenson name is not that of a unified family or clan, but is a common surname that has produced a list of great Scottish and international figures and its own tartan. One of the earliest recorded instances of the name appears in 1286, when one Ada Stephani (an early variant spelling) was listed as a burgess of Elgin. Later Stephanis took land charters in Ayr in the early fifteenth century, by which time the town of Stevenston, north Ayrshire, had been established by royal charter. There are numerous great Stevensons/Stephensons, including the writer Robert Louis Stevenson (1850–94) and the engineer George Stephenson (1781–1848), the pioneer of steam railway travel.

# Stewart of Appin

**Badge:** The head of a unicorn, with Scots motto *Quhidder will zie?* (Whither will ye?)

**Gaelic:** *Stiùbhartach na h-Apann*

The Clan Stewart, or Stuart, is undoubtedly the most powerful of all the Scottish clans. From this clan came a total of no fewer than 14 monarchs of Scotland and/or England. The origins of the clan lie with John Stewart of Bonkyl, a High Steward of Scotland in the twelfth century – the clan taking its name from his position. The Stewarts divided into several branches. The progenitor of this branch was Dougal Stewart (d. 1497), who avenged the muder of his father Sir John Stewart of Lorn at the hands of MacDougall outlaws, then led his kindred north from Lorn to Appin.

# Stewart of Atholl

*Badge:* The head of a unicorn, with Scots motto *Quhidder will zie?* (Whither will ye?)
*Gaelic:* Stiùbhartach Athall

The Stewart of Atholl branch is descended from Alexander Stewart (1343–1405), who was the Earl of Buchan. Alexander was a violent and fertile leader, whose many illegitimate offspring gave rise to several other branches of the Stewart family, including the Stewarts of Atholl. The key moment in Atholl history was when Sir James Stewart inherited the estates of the Earl of Atholl through marriage to James I's widow, after the earl was executed for his part in James's murder. The Stewart/Stuart of Atholl tartan should not be confused with Atholl's district sett.

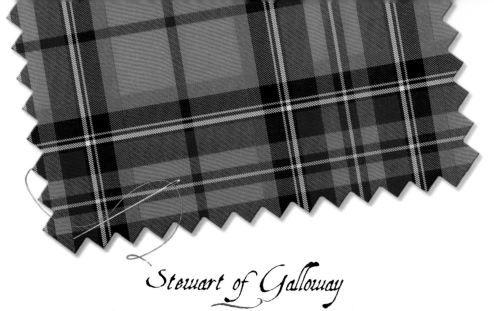

# Stewart of Galloway

*Badge:* Pelican feeding its young with its own blood, with Latin motto
*Virescit vulnere virtus* (Courage gains strength from a wound)
*Gaelic:* Stiùbhartach Ghall-Ghàidhealaibh

The Stewarts of Galloway claim direct descent from John Stewart of Bonkyl (*see* page 292), this branch of the clan being raised to the peerage in the seventeenth century. Today, the Galloway Stewarts are classed as the most senior branch of the Stewart family. Two tartans relate to the Stewarts of Galloway, both based on designs laid down in the first half of the nineteenth century. The sett here was established by Wilsons of Bannockburn in 1819, while the other sett was amongst drawings relating to the *Vestiarium Scoticum* of 1842.

# Stirling and Bannockburn

*Badge:* Saltire cross with a lion rampant in the centre and two caltraps and two spur rowels in the angles  *Gaelic:* Sruighlea agus Allt a' Bhonnaich

The Stirling and Bannockburn tartan was a district tartan designed by Wilsons of Bannockburn in their 1847 pattern book. It celebrates two of the most historically significant place names in Scottish history. At Stirling Bridge in 1297, William Wallace (d. 1305) defeated an invading English army, bringing Scotland a short period of independent rule before the next English onslaught. At Bannockburn in 1314, Robert the Bruce (r. 1306–29) inflicted a similar scathing defeat upon the army of Edward II (r. 1307–27), who was attempting to relieve the Scottish siege of Stirling Castle.

## Stone of Destiny

*Gaelic:* Clach Sgàin

The Stone of Destiny is an ancient symbol of Scottish identity, although much of its history has seen it in England. Legend has it that the stone was Jacob's pillow as he dreamed of angels ascending to heaven. Its ancestral home was Ireland, where it was used as a seat for crowning kings, as it was used when it was later transported to Scotland, finally coming to rest at Scone (hence its other name, the 'Stone of Scone'). It was taken by Edward I (r. 1272–1307) in 1296, and it sat in Westminster Abbey for the next 700 years until returned to Scotland in 1996, for which occasion this celebratory tartan was made.

# Stuart, Charles Edward

*Gaelic: Teàrlach Eideard Stiùbhart*

Charles Edward Stuart (1720–88), better known as Bonnie Prince Charlie, has been a particularly stirring and romantic figure in Scottish history. The son of James Stuart, the Old Pretender (1688–1766), Charles was born in Rome and later made a bid to retake the throne of Britain for the Stuarts, aided by Louis XV (r. 1715–74) of France. Landing in the Hebrides in 1745, Charles advanced through Scotland and south as far as Derby, until defeat at the Battle of Culloden (1746) ended his ambitions, and he fled to France. This tartan is actually based on a pair of trews apparently worn by Charles at Culloden.

## Sturrock

The first recorded member of the Clan Sturrock was one Layrence Sturrock, who served as the chaplain to Covil in 1453, and subsequently in Aberdeen. The Sturrocks appear to have hailed from Angus in the late Middle Ages, from the village of Craquhy near Dunnichen. Throughout history, the Sturrock name – which was traditionally said to mean 'stock farmer', or 'storemaster' – became spread throughout Scotland. Variant forms of the name include Storrack, Storek and Sturrach, and several Sturrocks have left their mark. Archibald Sturrock (1816–1909) was an important mechanical engineer, and Dr Peter Andrew Sturrock (b. 1924) became a prominent astrophysicist and President of the Society of Space Exploration.

# Sutherland

*Badge:* Cat, with French motto *Sans peur* (Without fear)  *Gaelic:* Sutharlanach

This clan is naturally connected to the territory of Sutherland, situated in the far north of Scotland, known by the early Norse settlers as Sudrland. The primary ancestor of the Sutherland chiefs was Freskin, who was also the progenitor of the Clan Murray. His descendants steadily gained lands throughout Sutherland, which became the location for the earliest earldom conferred in Britain, the honour going to William, Lord of Sutherland, in *c.* 1228. The clan became powerful through marital connections, but was also frequently at war, particularly with the Gunn and Mackay clans.

# Tartan Army

*Gaelic:* Airm a' Bhreacain

Although classified as 'Corporate', the Tartan Army sett is a visual ambassador of general Scottish identity. The 'Tartan Army' concept developed during the 1970s, the phrase being the invention of a sports journalist. It came to represent the good spirit and kilted attire of Scotland's football supporters during international tournaments, a compliment to both their patriotism and their friendliness towards rival fans. The actual tartan was designed in 1997 by Keith Lumsden of the Scottish Tartans Society, the sett combining the Royal Stewart tartan with that of the Black Watch as a background. Several regions, towns and cities have since created their own variant Tartan Army setts.

# Taylor

Badge: Five arrows, with Gaelic motto *Aonihn ri cheile* (All together as one)

Gaelic: Mac an Tàilleir

The first recorded Taylor ancestor is an Alexander le Taillur, who served as valet to Alexander III (r. 1249–86) from 1276. His surname clearly indicates Norman origins, it coming from the French *taileur*, meaning a 'cutter of cloth'. Nearly a dozen Taylors were later signatories of the oath of allegiance to Edward I (r. 1272–1307) in 1296. Clan tradition, however, often sees the progenitor as 'Black Tailor of the Axe', a sixteenth-century warrior and illegitimate son of a Cameron chief, hence the Taylors are regarded as a sept of the Camerons.

## Tweedside

The River Tweed has both a symbolic and a geographical importance to Scotland, providing an eastern boundary between Scotland and England, and also giving drainage to much of the Borders region. It flows into the North Sea at Berwick-upon-Tweed, having risen near the village of Tweedsmuir some 156 km (96 miles) inland. The Tweed was an important physical landmark during the Scottish Wars of Independence, and throughout history has also yielded plentiful salmon to the Border Scots. This district tartan was created by Wilsons of Bannockburn during the 1840s, in celebration of the life of the river. There is also a hunting variation of the sett, designed around the same time.

## Urquhart

*Badge:* Demi-otter, with Latin motto *Per mare per terras* (By sea and land)

*Gaelic:* Urchadan

Although one clan chief fancifully traced his ancestry back to Adam and Eve, the actual origins are more clearly identified in the fourteenth century. During the reign of Robert the Bruce (r. 1306–29), one William Urquhart, Sheriff of Cromarty, married a daughter of the Earl of Ross, and became a significant local landholder. The Urquharts were powerful around Cromarty, and also became the constables of Urquhart Castle on Loch Ness, built during the 1200s. The chieftainship of the Urquharts went dormant in 1898, but is today held in the United States.

## Wallace

*Badge:* Armoured arm gripping a sword, with Latin motto *Pro libertate sperandum est* (For liberty we hope) *Gaelic:* Uallas

The name Wallace derives from the word 'Wallensis', used by early medieval historians to describe the Britons of the Strathclyde region, which was a separate kingdom until the early eleventh century. During the twelfth century, the Wallace ancestors acquired lands throughout Renfrewshire and Ayrshire, and produced one of the greatest figures in Scottish history, Sir William Wallace (d. 1305). Wallace's long-running war against the English may have ended in his execution in London, but even today he remains an enduring symbol of Scottish independence.

## Weir

Badge: Boar on a cap of maintenance, with Latin motto *Vero nihil verius*
(Nothing is truer than the truth)

The Weir name is another Norman import, brought over to Scotland from the town of Ver, near Bayeux in Normandy. During the reign of William I of Scotland (r. 1165–1214), there is a record of one Ralph de Vere being captured at the Battle of Alnwick (1174), and he is traditionally seen as the ancestor of the Weir line, although it should be noted that, during the seventeenth century, many MacNairs also adopted the Weir surname. Both the Vere and Weir names live on in several tartans, the pattern seen here recorded in 1880.

# Wemyss

**Badge:** Swan, with French motto *Je pense* (I think)  **Gaelic:** Uamh

The name Wemyss derives from the Gaelic word for cave, *uaimh*, referring to the rugged coastline of Fife from where the Wemyss clan originates. The clan seat was, and remains, Wemyss Castle, built during the medieval period but destroyed by the vengeful English following the family's alliance with Robert the Bruce (r. 1306–29). The castle was rebuilt, and the clan's fortunes and landholdings improved, the clan chief becoming an earl in the 1630s. There is one Wemyss tartan, shown here, which was recorded in the *Vestiarium Scoticum* during the nineteenth century.

# Wilson

**Badge:** Demi-lion rampant, with Latin motto *Semper vigilans* (Ever watchful)

Wilson has become an extremely common name throughout the English-speaking world, but particularly so in Scotland. A search of the Scottish Register of Tartans under 'Wilson' produces 150 results, partly because of the association of the name with one of the greatest historical tartan makers, Wilsons of Bannockburn. Founded by William Wilson in the mid-eighteenth century, the company came to be the premier tartan maker in Scotland. The sett here was designed by William Wilson for his wife Janet, but was adopted as the Wilson famly/clan society in 1997.

# Wotherspoon

*Motto:* Deo juvante (By God's assistance)

The Wotherspoon name, more commonly found in its variants Witherspoon and Weatherspoon, dates back to at least the fourteenth century – one of the earliest ancestors recorded is a Roger Wythirspon of Renfrewshire. The family history is mainly concentrated in the Scottish Lowlands, and the name suggests agricultural origins, from the Old English *wedder* (sheep) and *spong* (pasture). During the eighteenth and nineteenth centuries, many of the family settled in North America, where the name became a significant presence with figures such as John Witherspoon (1722–94), a signatory on the Declaration of Independence.

## Wrens

'Wrens' was the shorthand for personnel of the Women's Royal Naval Service (WRNS), a branch of the Royal Navy that provided critical service from its foundation in 1916 until its absorption into the wider navy in 1993. (It was disbanded between 1919 and 1939.) The Wrens provided specialist services in many contrasting areas, including serving as cooks, wireless telegraphists, code experts, clerks and electricians. It led to the inclusion of women in ships' crews from 1990 and today women typically make up about a third of Royal Navy crews. The Wrens tartan was created in 1997 to commemorate the service and was designed by Peter MacDonald.

# Irish Tartans

## Antrim

**Badge:** Red lion rampant on a gold field, surmounted by a red hand flanked by towers, with Latin motto *Per angusta ad augusta* (Through trial to triumph)  **Gaelic:** Aontroim

The Antrim tartan is a trade and district tartan designed by MacNaughtons of Pitlochry, a producer of many Irish tartans. It was created for expat Irish living in Scotland, although it is also worn for ceremonial events in Ireland. Antrim, a county in the far north-east of Northern Ireland, has enjoyed a close relationship with Scotland on account of its geographical proximity. It was a launching point for the Scottish conquest of Dalriada in the fifth century, and later received large numbers of Scottish immigrants during the Tudor era.

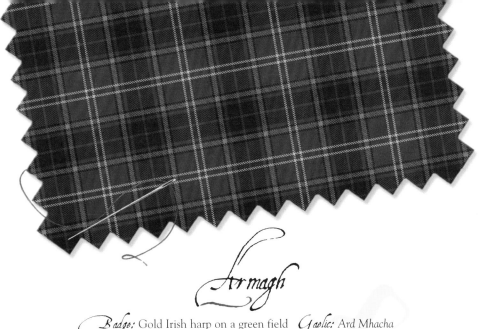

# Armagh

Badge: Gold Irish harp on a green field    Gaelic: Ard Mhacha

There are two tartans associated with the Northern Irish county of Armagh, one designed by Polly Wittering of the House of Edgar in the 1990s (seen here) and a later design set in very different colours by Viking Technology Limited. Although the Scottish Register of Tartans notes that 'Strictly speaking this [the tartan seen here] should be categorized as a "Fashion" tartan rather than a "District"', it is popular amongst those who celebrate the life of this ancient region. During the fifth century, St Patrick established Armagh as the centre of Irish Christianity, which it remains today.

## Carlow

**Badge:** Dimidiated lions rampant and couchant   **Gaelic:** Ceatharlach

County Carlow, located in the south-east of the Republic of Ireland in the province of Leinster, is centred on the town of Carlow. Evidence of human settlement dates back to at least the Stone Age, dramatically evidenced by megalithic structures such as the Brown Hill Dolmen, possibly a royal burial site. By the seventh century, monasteries were active in the county, although they suffered under later Viking depredations. The impressive Carlow Castle was constructed in the thirteenth century. The tartan here was designed by Polly Wittering of the House of Edgar, and registered in 1996.

## Cavan

**Badge:** Two gold balls on a blue field with a Crusader tent above and a green lion rampant below, with Irish motto *Feardhacht is Fírinne* (Manliness and truth)  **Gaelic:** An Cabhán

Located in the far north of the Republic of Ireland, County Cavan has been inhabited for at least five thousand years. During the Middle Ages, the county developed as a centre of Christian worship, expressed in locations such as Drumlane Monastery and Kilmore Cathedral. The synergy between Cavan and Scotland was particularly strong during the seventeenth century, when many Scottish planters settled in the county, developing towns such as Killeshandra and Virginia. Polly Wittering of the House of Edgar designed the tartan seen here in the 1990s.

# Clodagh

*Gaelic:* Clodagh

Clodagh is in County Cork, and it acquired its own tartan designed by D.C. Dalgleish at the beginning of the 1970s. The Scottish Register of Tartans notes that the sett is 'Said to have been based on a sample found in the Bog of Allen in Southern Ireland' (one hundred miles away), but it is almost identical to a tartan named Bowling, and very similar to a Royal Stewart tartan. To confuse matters further, a note attached with the Clodagh tartan also referred to it as 'Dowling', probably in reference to the man who found the sample.

## Connaught

**Badge:** Dimidiated spread eagle and an arm holding a sword   **Gaelic:** Connachta

The large western Irish province of Connaught contains the counties Galway, Leitrim, Mayo, Roscommon and Sligo, and was a major Celtic kingdom during the pre-Christian age. It retained its independent status for more than a thousand years, until it finally became part of the larger kingdom of Ireland in 1224. Connaught became the seat of a dukedom during the reign of Queen Victoria (r. 1837–1901), held by her son Prince Arthur (1850–1942). There are four tartans bearing the Connaught name, three designed in the 1990s and a sett of US origin registered in 2002.

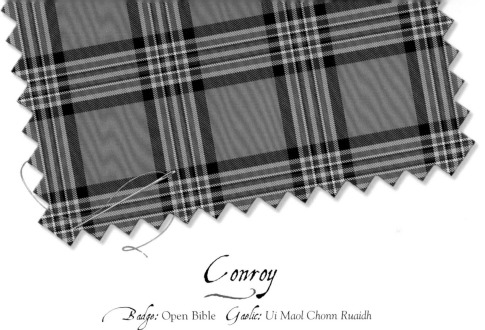

# Conroy

Badge: Open Bible  Gaelic: Ui Maol Chonn Ruaidh

The Conroy tartan is a personal tartan designed and registered during the 1980s by Leslie B. Conroy of Sydney, New South Wales, Australia. As a personal sett, it gives a particular family a tartan identity that links them to the wider community of Conroys. The Conroy name is an ancient one in Ireland, its main ancestral lands believed to be around the Galway Bay area. During the medieval period, several generations of Conroys served as bards to Irish kings, and literary connections continue with writers such as American author Frank Conroy (1936–2005).

# Cork

**Badge:** Two towers bearing the Cross of St Patrick, either side of a sailing ship **Gaelic:** Corcaigh

County Cork sits at the extreme south of the Republic of Ireland, but has had a central role in Ireland's history. Cork, the second largest city in the Republic, was founded during the seventh century by St Finnbarr. The county fell under English control in the early twelfth century, but its resistant nature during the Wars of the Roses (1455–85) earned it the title 'The Rebel County' from its English overlords. It was also a major stronghold of the Irish Republican Army (IRA) during the Irish Civil War of 1922–23.

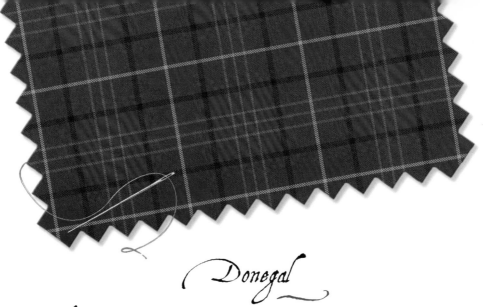

## Donegal

**Badge:** Red cross-crosslet on a white shield set within wavy bands of green and gold

**Gaelic:** Tír Chonaill

Evidence from megalithic stone circles and ancient hill forts indicates that County Donegal was settled by at least 3000 BC. Grianán of Aileach, a ring fort with origins in the early Iron Age, was the residence of the Uí Neill, the High Kings of Ireland in the fifth century, and later the seat of the chieftains of Donegal, the O'Donnells, a dominant force in Ireland until the seventeenth century. Later history subdued the county – it was devastated by the famine of the 1840s, and it was blighted by violence during the Troubles of the 1960s–90s.

## Down

**Badge:** Three wheat sheaves, a fish and a sailing ship, with Latin motto
*Absque labore nihil* (Nothing without labour) **Gaelic:** *Contae an Dún*

County Down's vivid history lives on in numerous monuments and buildings, from Stone Age standing stones to impressive fortifications built by the Anglo-Normans and British. The County Down name derives from the Gaelic *Dún Pádraig*, which means 'the stronghold of St Patrick' – St Patrick's first church was, according to tradition, built in County Down, on the site of the ruins of Saul Abbey. The County Down tartan was another inspiring 1990s design by Polly Wittering of the House of Edgar, and is gradually attaining the status of a district sett.

# Doyle

*Badge:* Various, but commonly three stags' heads   *Gaelic:* Dubh gall

The Gaelic rendering of Doyle means 'dark foreigner', distinguishing the clan's dark-haired Danish Viking descendants from the blonde-haired (*fionn gall*) Vikings from Norway. Although the progenitor of the clan is uncertain, some authorities give it as the Norse noble Dubh Gilla, who settled in Ireland in the year 851. Doyles are today found across the world, and this tartan was registered by the Australia-based Clan Doyle Society, which explains the tartan colours as 'Green for its Irishness, Red for the warlike Danish Vikings, Gold for glory and wealth'.

## Dublin

**Badge:** Three burning castles, with Latin motto *Obedientia civium urbis felicitas* (Happy the city where citizens obey)   **Gaelic:** *Baile Átha Cliath*

Before the arrival of the Anglo-Normans in 1171, Dublin was periodically dominated by Viking settlers, although Irish rebels ensured that the Norsemen were forced to fight for their occupation. The city remained fairly small until the seventeenth century, when it was occupied by Oliver Cromwell and began a long period of commercial and population growth. From the early nineteenth century, Dublin was the site of the struggle against the Anglo-Irish Act of Union, which led to outright war and the independence of the Irish Free State (later the Republic of Ireland) in 1921.

## Fermanagh

**Badge:** Fortification flying the Cross of St Patrick over blue and white waves
**Gaelic:** Fear Manach

Three tartans relate to County Fermanagh, part of the province of Ulster in Northern Ireland. The first is listed as 'Fermanagh (1990)', based upon the muted colours of a tartan rug discovered in 1990. This pattern was possibly the inspiration for the 1996 district tartan, designed by Polly Wittering of the House of Edgar. Another set was released in 2005 by Viking Technology Limited, the colours based on those of the county's heraldic arms. The castle on these arms represents the old fortification between the Upper and Lower Erne, Enniskillen, held by the Maguires, Kings of Fermanagh.

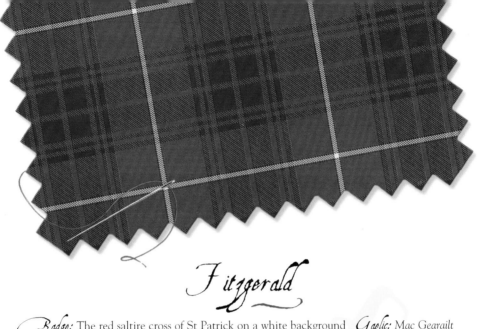

# Fitzgerald

**Badge:** The red saltire cross of St Patrick on a white background **Gaelic:** Mac Gearailt

Fitzgerald is a particularly resonant name in Ireland, belonging to what was once one of the most powerful clans in the land. They arrived around the time of the Norman Conquest in the eleventh century, the traditional progenitor being Walter, son of Other, who sired Gerald – the prefix 'Fitz' comes from the French word *fils* (son). The focal points of Fitzgerald power were in Leinster and Munster, where the Fitzgeralds came to hold several earldoms. Three Fitzgeralds have held the position of Taoiseach, Prime Minister of Ireland.

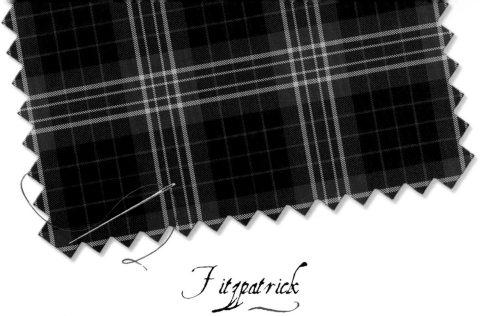

# Fitzpatrick

**Badge:** Three gold fleur-de-lys over the Cross of St Andrew   **Gaelic:** MacGiolla Phádraig

The Fitzpatricks, like the Fitzgeralds (*see* page 325), were another exceptionally powerful Irish family with a long ancestry. The Gaelic name means 'Son of the servant of St Patrick', and the 'Fitz' element is actually of Irish rather than Norman origin. The progenitor is traditionally held to be Giolla Pádraig, a tenth-century chief of the ancient Irish kingdom of Ossory. There are two Fitzpatrick tartans registered, one (seen here) created in the early 1990s from a 1970s American sample, and the plainer and darker 'Fitzpatrick Hunting' of 2002, both similar to the Cameron of Erracht pattern.

## Galway

**Badge:** Gold lion rampant in a blue shield on a sailing ship, with Gaelic motto *Ceart agus Cóir* (Righteousness and justice) **Gaelic:** *Gaillimh*

In terms of the first inhabitants of County Galway, there is evidence of human settlement dating back to 5000 BC. Galway city had its beginnings in the early twelfth century AD, but was officially founded in the thirteenth century. The following century saw the city achieve royal borough status, and it became known internationally for its exports of wool, hides and leather, while it was also a major centre for the import of wine. Although it periodically suffered from war, plague and famine, Galway has maintained growth and prosperity to this day.

## Irish National

*Badge:* Gold harp shaped as a winged female, with Gaelic motto *Erin gu bragh* (Ireland for ever)

*Gaelic:* Éire

The Irish National sett was designed as a tartan that can be worn by anyone of Irish descent, anywhere in the world. Its design came about through an act of international co-operation, the Scottish Register of Tartans noting that it was 'Conceived and designed by Polly Wittering of the House of Edgar in association with John and Joan (Jo) Nisbet of Piper's Cove in New Jersey USA'. (Piper's Cove is a major US importer of Scottish and Irish goods.) It is a fine tartan, much in evidence in American St Patrick's Day parades.

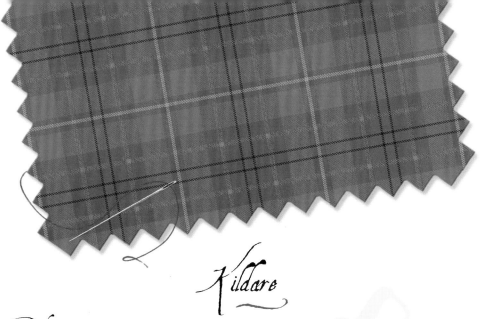

# Kildare

**Badge:** Saint Brigid's Cross, a sprig of oak, a harp and a horse's head, displayed around crossed swords, with Irish motto *Meanma agus Misneach* (Spirit and courage)   **Gaelic:** *Cill Dara*

The sprig of oak in the County Kildare coat of arms refers to the oak tree in which St Brigid (*c.* 450–525) built her cell. As founder of a convent in Kildare (and three elsewhere), Brigid is particularly important to the historical identity of the county, but she was also highly influential in Scotland, especially in the west of the country and the Hebrides. County Kildare began its recorded life in the Christian Middle Ages, with the county receiving its first monastery in the late fifth century.

# Kilkenny

*Badge:* Dimidiated arms displaying three wheat sheaves and three knots   *Gaelic:* Cill Chainnigh

The Gaelic for Kilkenny, *Cill Chainnigh*, translates as 'Church of St Canice' or 'St Kenny'. Canice (c. 515–600) was born at Glenliven, County Derry, the son of a well-known bard. As a young man, he felt a divine calling, and became a priest in Glamorganshire, Wales, in 545 (he had met Welsh Christian leaders while studying in Dublin). His religious journey took Canice to Rome and Scotland and back to Ireland, and in Kilkenny he is known for the monastery he established at Drumachose.

## Laois

**Badge:** Two gold lions on a red background, over two gold fleur-de-lys on a blue background, with Irish motto *I bpáirt leis an bpobal* (In partnership with the community) **Gaelic:** Laois

The very name of Laois, a county located in the province of Leinster in the central Republic of Ireland, tells a history. From 1556 until 1922, this territory was known as Queen's County, named in honour of Mary Tudor (r. 1553–58), its principal town Maryborough. In the wake of the Irish War of Independence (1919–21), the Queen's County name naturally had an unwanted resonance, and Laois was adopted instead, Maryborough becoming Port Laois. This tartan was designed in the 1990s, courtesy of Polly Wittering of the House of Edgar.

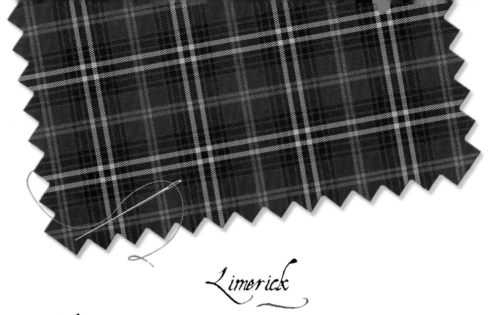

## Limerick

*Badge:* Gold cross pattee in a gold circle on three vertical undulating lines on a green background, with Irish motto *Cuimhnigh ar Luimneach* (Remember Limerick)  *Gaelic: Luimneach*

The foundations for the city of Limerick date back to at least the ninth century and, during the Middle Ages, the city flourished, notwithstanding the effects of frequent wars that rolled through the region. Major historical features in the county include King John's Castle, built in 1210 as a stamp of Norman authority, and St Mary's Cathedral, which was completed in 1194 (three years later, Limerick was given the charter declaring it a city). The Limerick County tartan is another creation of the 1990s.

# *Londonderry*

*Badge:* Two wheat sheaves flanking a white rose over a red hand, with Latin motto
*Auxilium a domino* (Help comes from the Lord)  *Gaelic:* Doire

Also known as Derry, the county of Londonderry in Ulster sits in the far north of Ireland. The 'London' prefix was added by the English in the early seventeenth century, when the county and city of Derry were given to the City of London as part of ongoing English settlement policy. Today, the county and city are known by both names, the usage usually split along loyalist and republican lines. Derry comes from the Gaelic *Doire*, which means 'oak grove', a reference to the geophysical features of the region.

## Manx Laxey Red

*Badge:* Three legs, joined, booted and spurred, with Latin motto *Quocunque ieceris stabit* (Whichever way you throw it, it will stand) *Gaelic:* Laksey Ruagh Manninagh

The Isle of Man has inspired no fewer than 13 tartans. The island itself is an unusual place in the British Isles; it is a self-governing Crown dependency, in the sea between Ireland, Scotland and England. (More of the history of the Isle of Man is covered in the next entry.) The tartan seen here is a district sett designed in the early 1980s. Other Manx tartans include Manx Laxey Dress Green, Manx Mannin Plaid and Manx Heritage, the last designed by the Manx Museum in 1998 as a corporate tartan.

# Manx National

*Badge:* Three legs, joined, booted and spurred, with Latin motto *Quocunque ieceris stabit* (Whichever way you throw it, it will stand) *Gaelic:* Ashoonagh Manninagh

The Isle of Man, owing to its location, has been influenced by the cultures of England, Scotland and Ireland. It was settled by the Vikings from the eighth century (although evidence of earlier settlements goes back to 5000 BC), but was taken into Scottish then English hands during the thirteenth century. The island belonged to various English lords and authorities until 1765, when it was purchased by the British government, although its system of governance was not incorporated into Britain's. The Manx National tartan was designed in the 1940s by Miss Patricia McQuaid.

## Mayo

**Badge:** White saltire cross on a red background, displaying five crosses, with a castle, green trees and crossed battle-axes, with Irish motto *Dia is Muire Linn* (God and Mary be with us)

**Gaelic:** Mhaigh Eo

County Mayo is in the province of Connaught on the west coast of Ireland. The county gave rise to the Earl of Mayo peerage, which was created in 1785 for John Bourke (1705–90), who served as the First Commissioner of Revenue in Ireland. (The position of Viscount Mayo had been established in 1629.) Subsequent earls of Mayo were heavily involved in both British and Irish politics. The Mayo tartan was a Polly Wittering design for the House of Edgar. Another Mayo tartan is available, rendered in the county's heraldic colours.

## Meath

*Badge:* King, with crown and sceptre, seated on a throne, with Irish motto
*Neart le Chéile* (Together strong)  *Gaelic:* Midhe

What we today call County Meath was, until the late twelfth century, part of a larger independent kingdom, ruled by its own royal court. This kingdom occupied much of the modern province of Leinster but, in 1173, Hugh de Lacy of Leinster (*c.* 1135–86) was granted the lordship of Meath by Henry II (*r.* 1154–89). Stone Age ruins, ancient monuments and monastic houses are found throughout the county. One of its most popular tourist sites is the Hill of Tara that, according to legend, was the seat of the High Kings of Ireland.

## O'Brien

*Badge:* Three lions passant gardant, half gold, half white, on a red background, with Irish motto
*Lamh laidir in uachtar* (Strong arm uppermost) *Gaelic:* Ui Briain

The O'Brien dynasty has an impeccable Irish ancestry. Its progenitor was Brian Boru (941–1014), Prince of Thomond (North Munster), chief of the Dalgais and, in 1002, the High King of Ireland. Brian was killed in 1014 while fighting the Danes at Clontarf, but he established a powerful line in Irish history. The family received the barony of Inchiquin in 1543, which then became a baronetcy in 1686. One of the O'Brien tartans currently registered includes two red lines, one for each of Brian Boru's major battle victories.

## O'Connor

*Badge:* Green tree on a white background    *Gaelic:* Ui Conaire

The O'Connor name is one of the commonest Irish surnames, both at home and abroad. They are descended from the medieval kings of Connaught, with six distinct branches of the family surviving into modern times. The Connaught branch remains the most important, and is in turn separated into the O'Connor Don, O'Connor Roe and O'Connor Sligo septs. There have been numerous famous O'Connors throughout history, including the leader of the Chartist movement, Feargus O'Connor (1794–1855) and Sandra Day O'Connor, the first female to sit on the US Supreme Court.

## O'Neill

*Badge:* The red hand of Ulster flanked by facing red lions rampant, with Irish motto
*Lám dearg Éirinn* (The red hand of Ireland)　*Gaelic:* Uí Néill

The O'Neill name stretches back into the fourth century AD, its earliest ancestors generally regarded as the sons of Niall Naoi Ghiallach (Niall of the Nine Hostages), the High King of Ireland from 377 to 404. Such ancient origins are attested by the clan's badge, which features a red hand that was displayed on standards in pagan times. The red hand symbol is also the motif of the province of Ulster, where the O'Neills are most numerous, but there are also large concentrations of the clan in counties Clare, Limerick, Decies, Waterford and Carlow.

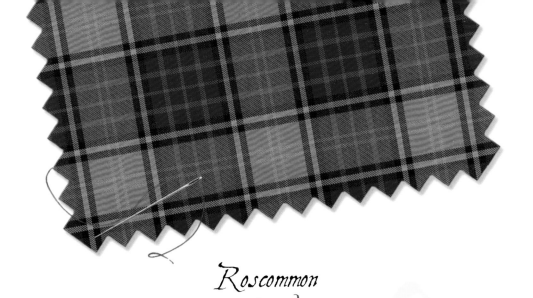

## Roscommon

**Badge:** Gold 'V' enclosing a green field displaying a gold cross pattee and crown, flanked by a ram's head and a sprig of shamrock, with Latin motto *Constans Hiberniae Cor* (Steadfast Irish heart)

**Gaelic:** Ros Comáin

County Roscommon sits almost in the dead centre of Ireland, in the province of Connacht. The name translates as 'the wooded heights of St Coman', the saint being the first bishop of the See of Roscommon, in the eighth century. Coman not only founded a monastery in Roscommon, but also wrote the 'Law of Coman', an influential monastic rule that was still in use by the late medieval period amongst Augustinians and other sects. The Coman name is still very evident in the county today, used for institutions ranging from churches to bars.

## Tara (Murphy)

**Badge:** Four lions rampant, divided by a black band featuring three gold wheat sheaves

**Gaelic:** Teamhair (Uí Mhurchú)

The Hill of Tara, dating back to megalithic times, is one of Ireland's most spiritually charged locations. Tradition has it as the seat of the High King of Ireland in the pre-Christian Age – the pillar stone known as the 'Stone of Destiny' is believed to be the site on which the kings of Ireland were crowned. (Many Irish believe the stone never left Ireland for Scotland.) The Tara tartan shown here was originally described as the sett of the Clan Murphy in the *Clans Originaux* (1880), but it was applied to Tara during the 1960s.

# Tipperary

*Badge:* On a field or ermine, a band alternating blue, red and gold bearing two sets of three cups

*Gaelic:* Tiobraid Arann

Tipperary is a large county in the province of Munster. Established during the thirteenth century, Tipperary is actually one of the oldest of the Irish counties, and grew into such a large area that it is today divided into two administrative districts, North and South Tipperary. The Tipperary name is taken from the Gaelic *Tiobraid Arann*, which means 'the well of the [River] Ara'. The tartan seen here is another design from Polly Wittering of the House of Edgar, one of a series of Irish district tartans created in the 1990s.

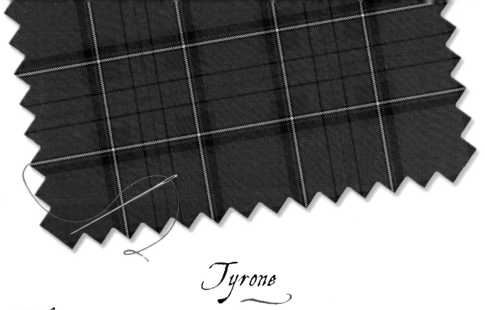

## Tyrone

**Badge:** The red hand of Ulster on a white background surmounted by a blue band displaying a fleur-de-lys, with Latin motto *Consilio et prudentia* (By wisdom and prudence) **Gaelic:** *Tír Eoghain*

The Gaelic for Tyrone, *Tír Eoghain*, translates as 'The land of the Eoghan', referring to a son of Niall of the Nine Hostages (*see* page 340). Today, it is the largest county in Northern Ireland; before a territorial carve-up in the seventeenth century, it also included part of County Londonderry. In 1542, Conn O'Neill (*c.* 1480–1559) became the 1st Earl of Tyrone, a peerage title that was recreated on two more occasions before becoming defunct at the end of the eighteenth century. The County Tyrone tartan was registered in 1996.

## Ulster

*Badge:* Red cross on a gold field, with a white shield bearing the red hand in the centre

*Gaelic:* Cúige Uladh

The province of Ulster encompasses six counties of Northern Ireland and three counties of the Republic of Ireland. Ulster's history is a bloody one, its people caught amidst sectarianism, faith and colonization, and it was a battleground for the Troubles of the late 1960s–late 1990s. It has acquired more tartans than many Irish counties (five at the time of writing). The Ulster (Red) sett shown here is based upon fabric discovered in a bog in Flanders Townland near Dungiven, County Londonderry, 1956 and dates back to the sixteenth century.

## Waterford

*Badge:* Tower flanked by an eagle's head with three ears of wheat in its mouth, a stag's head with the Cross of Saint Hubert, above a lymphad, with Irish motto *Déisi oc Declán co bráth* (May the Déise remain with Declan for ever)   *Gaelic:* Port Láirge

County Waterford is in Munster on the south-east coast of Ireland. From the sixth century, like many of Ireland's counties, it became a place of religious worship for sects such as the Augustinians, Cistercians, Dominicans and even the Knights Templar. Evidence of this past is seen in the abbeys of Molana, Mount Melleray, Rincrew and many others. The tartan is another offering from Polly Wittering of the House of Edgar – this company was founded in Edinburgh in the nineteenth century, later moving to Pitlochry then Perth.

# Westmeath

*Badge:* Saltire divided into blue and red, bearing a gold ring flanked by gold lions rampant, with a swan above and a horned helmet below, with Irish motto *Triath ós triathaibh* (Noble above nobility)  *Gaelic:* An Iarmhí

Westmeath was created when the province of Meath was divided up in the sixteenth century, and is part of the province of Leinster. Replete with historical ruins, particularly defensive, family estates and ecclesiastical structures, the county is today a popular tourist destination. One interesting feature is Uisneagh Hill, the place where King Tuathal Teachmar is said to have established his palace in the second century. Also impressive is Athlone Castle, built in 1210 by John de Gray, Bishop of Norwich, for King John (*r.* 1199–1216).

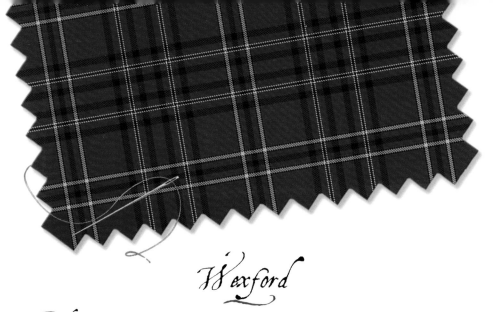

## Wexford

*Badge:* Three lymphads on a white background, with Latin motto *Exemplar Hiberniae* (An example to Ireland)  *Gaelic:* Loch Garman

Wexford became a county during the reign of King John (r. 1199–1216). Before this time, the territory flowed through the hands of the indigenous Irish, the Vikings and the Anglo-Normans. In later history, Wexford was a centre for the Irish Rebellion of 1798, the rebels suffering a critical defeat at the hands of the British at Vinegar Hill. The battle there became a landmark event in Irish republicanism. The county's Abercromby Monument remembers Sir Ralph Abercromby (1734–1801), British commander-in-chief forced to resign after complaining over the treatment of the Irish.

## Wicklow

*Badge:* Gold lion on a blue field over a Celtic church on a green field, with Irish motto *Meanma saor* (Free spirits) *Gaelic:* Cill Mhantáin

County Wicklow was founded in 1606, having previously been parts of County Carlow and County Dublin. It is a rugged county, and the Wicklow Mountains form dramatic scenery across the region – historically, they provided opportunities for mining gold and various other precious metals. An interesting feature of the county is the Military Road, a 55-km (34-mile) highway built through the Wicklow Mountains between 1800 and 1801 by the British to help them control Irish insurgency – today, the road is classified as the R115.

# *Index*

Page references in **bold** refer to the main article, which includes an illustration of the tartan and a description of the badge.